CONTENTS

5

ILLUSTRATIONS

Between Pages 96 and 97

Grand-Admiral Räder
Admiral Schniewind

Sealion Objectives—
The English coast from Brighton to Hythe

The German Surface Fleet,
   September 1940

Barge Assemblies, September 1940

The British Admirals

British Warships—1
British Warships—11

The Silent Victory

SEPTEMBER 1940

Duncan Grinnell-Milne

'In Britain, whatever our shortcomings, we understood the sea affair very thoroughly ... It was this above all things which enabled us to regard the menace of invasion with a steady gaze.'

Winston Churchill : *The Second World War*

WHITE LION PUBLISHERS LIMITED
London, Sydney and Toronto

First published in Great Britain
by The Bodley Head Ltd, 1958

Copyright © Duncan Grinnell-Milne, 1958

White Lion edition, 1976

ISBN 7274 0153 X

Made and printed in Great Britain
for White Lion Publishers Limited,
138 Park Lane, London W1Y 3DD
by Hendington Limited,
Deadbrook Lane, Aldershot, Hampshire

Acknowledgments

AND A WARNING

FIRST the warning: this is not intended to be a comprehensive history of all the military, political and economic considerations governing the events of 1939–40, but only so much of them as is necessary to make clear the maritime situation and to justify the claims of sea power. Although the argument might have been further developed, and other sources quoted to support it, it has seemed to me that enough has been set down in the following pages to prove the validity of the views expressed and that additional evidence would but make the narrative tedious.

With this in mind, I have attempted to discover only what the principal participants on either side thought or did at the time and upon what past experience they could rely in making their decisions. I have therefore omitted all discussion of subsequent happenings with which, in any event, there can be little worthwhile comparison.

For the capture of Crete in May 1941, for instance, the Germans were able to employ a force of air transports, gliders and parachute troops which was not available to them in September 1940 and which, barely sufficient for the task of overrunning a Greek island devoid of all the essentials for protracted defence, would have been quite inadequate for the conquest of Britain. It is worth remembering, however, that whereas the *airborne* assault was only just successful – and might have been wholly unsuccessful had stronger defences been built up a little earlier – not one man was landed from the *seaborne* invasion fleet which, despite the enemy's desperate attempts to protect it, was annihilated by the Royal Navy.

As for Normandy, 1944, there is even less ground for serious comparison. Plans and technical preparations for the return to France were in the making for the better part of four years; for *Sealion* they were accomplished in a matter of six weeks. And, aside from the manifold special services – the highly-developed landing-craft, the Mulberry harbours, the submarine pipeline from England to France – Anglo-American supremacy at sea was unchallengeable by a German Navy whose effective strength in the Channel area had dwindled to a score or two of motor torpedo-boats and a handful of midget submarines.

Even looking back into the past, from the standpoint of 1940, the events of comparatively recent history would offer no useful basis for comparison. The Gallipoli campaign could but serve as a reminder that the landings there were achieved by means of an allied naval power that, in the Aegean, was undisputed.

On the other hand, it is vain to suggest that in 1940 the Germans might have brought off an attack comparable to that made by the Japanese in 1941. The German Navy then possessed scarcely a dozen serviceable torpedo-bombers; its few aircraft were under the operational control of the Luftwaffe; and the Luftwaffe had no plan for their use. Nor was there, in British home waters, a single concentrated force whose partial destruction would have had an immediate strategic effect comparable to that of Pearl Harbour. Total surprise was out of the question.[1]

The story of *Sealion* must therefore be judged upon its own merits and demerits. Interest in it is not purely academic; it contains lessons which may well be valuable in the future – though not, one may hope, only to a potential enemy. But as an attempt to conquer these islands by seaborne invasion it must take its place with the other unsuccessful attempts of the past.

For 'attempt' there was – not just a plan – from the moment when the transports steamed from German harbours to assemble in the Channel ports, just as much as when the Armada sailed from Corunna towards Parma waiting in Flanders or as when, with Napoleon's Army encamped at Boulogne, the French Fleet sailed from Toulon on the first leg of the Trafalgar campaign. It is the purpose of the present work to show how this latest attempt was frustrated, and by whom.

To the Lords Commissioners of the Admiralty I would express

[1] It will be recalled that, for the successful attack on the *Prince of Wales* and *Repulse* (December 10th, 1941), the Japanese employed a highly specialized force of more than 30 bombers and 50 torpedo-carrying aircraft. No such force was available to Germany in September 1940.

my gratitude for their permission to consult the official documents and records which have enabled me to check and to amplify facts and figures obtained from many sources. At the same time I would like to offer my thanks to the Historical Section at the Admiralty – to Commander Kemp, its head, and to Commanders Rowbotham and Titterton amongst others – for much help given in searching through Memoranda, War diaries and 'Pink Lists'.

For a study of the invasion plan and its attempted execution one source is, as all authorities have found, indispensable: the German naval archives captured intact at the end of the war. Copious extracts, containing all the relevant facts and entitled *Führer Conferences on Naval Affairs*, were released by the Admiralty in 1947, printed by H.M. Stationery Office, and reprinted in Brassey's Naval Annual for 1948, published by Sampson Low, Marston & Co. From this material, which is Crown Copyright, I have had permission to quote extensively.

For the study of maritime affairs during the first year of war and, in particular, during the crucial period of 1940, I have relied largely upon the various sources and authorities listed below. In order to avoid a tiresome multiplicity of footnotes to the text I have marked with an asterisk those works upon which the account is based or from which passages have been quoted.

I wish to express my thanks to the Controller, H.M. Stationery Office, for permission to print extracts from the *Führer Conferences*, brief passages from Captain Roskill's *The War at Sea, Vol. I*, and from Basil Collier's *Defence of the United Kingdom*, and also passages quoted by Basil Collier in *Leader of the Few* (Jarrolds).

I am indebted to Eberhard Brockhaus, of Wiesbaden, for permission to quote from Admiral Assmann's work *Deutsche Schicksalsjahre*, to Messrs. Cassell for their permission to quote from Sir Winston Churchill's *The Second World War*, to Messrs. Collins for a few lines taken from Lord Alanbrooke's Diaries and quoted by Sir Arthur Bryant in *The Turn of the Tide*, to Messrs. Cassell for opinions quoted by Captain B. A. Liddell Hart in *The Other Side of the Hill*.

Personal acknowledgments are also due. First, to Admiral

of the Fleet the Earl of Cork and Orrery who was kind enough to read the typescript when it was heavily overscored with corrections, and whose approval gave me great encouragement. Secondly, to my old friend R. T. Clark, wartime chief of B.B.C. News, whose advice based upon a vast knowledge of political and military history was most helpful. Thirdly, to Admiral the Hon. Sir R. Plunkett-Ernle-Erle-Drax for his comments quoted in Appendix B.

I would also like to thank Mr H. Sampson, of Sampson Low & Marston, for his kindness in producing, at short notice, the silhouettes of German and photographs of British warships.

Sources

Sources from which passages are quoted in the text (marked*), authorities consulted, and other works useful to a study of the period, of the German invasion attempt and of naval affairs generally.

*Admiralty Hydrographic Department, *The Channel Pilot: Part 1*, (13th Edn, 1947)

*Assmann, Admiral Kurt (German Navy), *Deutsche Schicksalsjahre*, (Eberhard Brockhaus, Wiesbaden, 1951)

*Bryant, Sir Arthur, *The Turn of the Tide*, (Collins, 1957)

Bullock, Alan, *Hitler – A Study in Tyranny*, (Odhams, 1952)

Childers, Erskine, *The Riddle of the Sands*, (Sidgwick & Jackson, 1903)

*Churchill, Winston, *The Second World War, Vol. II*, (Cassell, 1949)

Churchill, Winston, *World Crisis – 1911–14*, (Thornton Butterworth, 1923)

Ciano, Count G., *Ciano's Diary*, (Heinemann, 1946)

*Collier, Basil, *Defence of the U.K. 1939–45* (Official War History Series), (H.M.S.O., 1957)

*Collier, Basil, *Leader of the Few*, (Jarrolds, 1957)

Corbett, Sir Julian, *Some Principles of Maritime Strategy*, (Longmans, 1918)

Corbett, Sir Julian, *Naval Operations Vol. I* (Official War History 1914–18), (Longmans, 1920)

Fleming, Peter, *Invasion 1940*, (Hart-Davis, 1957)

Führer Conferences on Naval Affairs, Ed. Anthony Martienssen, (H.M.S.O. and Brassey's Naval Annual, 1948, published by Sampson Low, Marston & Co.)

Fuller, Major-General, *The Second World War*, (Eyre & Spottiswoode, 1948)

*German Broadcasts, 1940

Grinnell-Milne, George, *Life of Admiral de Ruyter*, (Kegan Paul, Trench & Co., London, 1896)

*Hart, Captain B. H. Liddell, *The Other Side of the Hill*, (Cassell, 1951)

HINSLEY, F. H., *Hitler's Strategy*, (Cambridge University Press, 1951)

Jane's Fighting Ships, (Sampson Low, Marston & Co., 1939)

KEMP, Commander P. K., R.N., *H.M. Destroyers*, (Jenkins, 1956)

KEMP, Commander P. K., R.N., *H.M. Submarines*, (Jenkins, 1952)

KEMP, Commander P. K., R.N., *The Fleet Air Arm*, (Jenkins, 1954)

LLOYD'S, London, *Lloyd's Shipping Lists*, (1939)

MAHAN, Captain A. T., U.S.N., *The Influence of Sea Power Upon History*, (Sampson Low, Marston & Co., 1889)

MAHAN, Captain A. T., U.S.N., *Life of Nelson*, (Sampson Low, Marston & Co., 1897)

MANSTEIN, General von, *Verlorene Siege*, (Bonn, 1955)

*MARTIENSSEN, Anthony, *Hitler and His Admirals*, (Secker & Warburg, 1948)

MEDLICOTT, W. N., *The Economic Blockade, Vol. I* (Official War History Series), (H.M.S.O., 1952)

PILE, General Sir F., *Ack-Ack*, (Harrap, 1949)

*ROSKILL, Captain S. W., R.N., *The War at Sea, Vol. I* (Official War History Series), (H.M.S.O., 1954)

RUGE, Admiral Carl (German Navy), *Sea Warfare, 1939-45*, (Cassell, 1957)

SCOTT, Peter, 'The Battle of the Narrow Seas', *Country Life*, 1945

SHIRER, William L., *Berlin Diary*, (Hamish Hamilton, 1941)

SLESSOR, Marshal of the Royal Air Force, Sir J., *The Central Blue* (Cassell, 1956)

TIRPITZ, Grand-Admiral von, *My Memories*, (Hurst & Blackett, 1920)

*WEICHOLD, Admiral Eberhard (German Navy). Extract from a post-war Appreciation (see Appendix B)

WILMOT, Chester, *The Struggle for Europe*, (Collins, 1952)

Strength and disposition of Warships, incidents of Naval Operations, etc., are quoted from Admiralty records.

THE SILENT VICTORY

Prologue: Directive 16[1]

ALL AT ONCE the High Command of the German Army wanted to march against England.

It had seemed unthinkable before 1940; now it looked almost easy. Whilst the battle raged in France all thoughts had been held by the developing miracle of unimagined victory; at the end of June the new prospect suddenly glowed with such glorious possibility that the French armistice agreement had hardly been signed before the great project was being discussed, its details studied and a rough plan prepared at the Führer's command.

A secret plan, but all the world perceived the alternatives. Under the weight of overwhelming defeat upon the continent, Britain might fall into the snare of tempting peace offers. Or, accepting the challenge, she might rashly defy the irresistible assault of apparently invincible force. By Hitler, though he expected the first, both possibilities were considered so nearly simultaneously that when, by mid-July, Britain's choice had become disappointingly clear to him the alternative to negotiated surrender was ready to be communicated to the three fighting services.

The Führer and	Führer's Headquarters
Supreme Commander	July 16th, 1940
of the Armed Forces	

TOP SECRET   DIRECTIVE No. 16

Preparations for the Invasion of England

As England, in spite of the hopelessness of her military position, has so far shown herself unwilling to come to any compromise, I have therefore decided to begin to prepare for,

[1] The Directive is given here in full because study of it makes easier an understanding of all subsequent additions, developments and modifications to the *Sealion* plan. The text of this Directive, as of all passages quoted from the *Führer Naval Conferences*, will be found in *Brassey's Naval Annual* for 1948, published by Sampson Low, Marston & Co.

and if necessary to carry out, an invasion of England. This operation is dictated by the necessity of eliminating Great Britain as a basis from which the war against Germany can be fought and, if necessary, the island will be occupied.

I therefore issue the following orders:

¶ 1. The landing operation must be a surprise crossing on a broad front extending approximately from Ramsgate to a point west of the Isle of Wight. Units[1] of the Air Force will do the work of the artillery and units[1] of the Navy the work of engineers. I ask each of the fighting services to consider the advantage from their respective points of view of preliminary operations such as the occupation of the Isle of Wight or the Duchy of Cornwall prior to the full-scale invasion, and to inform me of the result of their deliberations. I shall be responsible for the final decision. The preparations for the large-scale invasion must be concluded by the middle of August.

¶ 2. The following preparations must be undertaken to make a landing in England possible:

(a) The British Air Force must be eliminated to such an extent that it will be incapable of putting up any substantial opposition to the invading troops.

(b) The sea routes must be cleared of mines.

(c) Both flanks of the Straits of Dover, and the Western Approaches to the Channel approximately on a line from Alderney to Portland, must be so heavily mined as to be completely inaccessible.

(d) Heavy guns must dominate and protect the entire coastal front area.

(e) It is desirable that the English fleets both in the North Sea and in the Mediterranean should be pinned down (by the Italians in the latter instance) shortly before the crossing takes place; with this aim in view, the naval forces at present in British harbours and coastal waters should be attacked from the air and by torpedoes.

[1] In the British version the word 'elements' is used. 'Units', in the American version, seems more appropriate.

¶ 3. Organization of the Commands and of the preparations.

The Commanders-in-Chief of the respective branches of the armed forces will lead their forces, under my orders. The Army, Navy and Air Force General Staffs should be within an area of no more than 50 km from my Headquarters (Ziegenberg) by August 1st. I suggest that the Army and Navy General Staffs establish their headquarters at Giessen.

The Commander-in-Chief of the Army will nominate an army group to lead the invasion forces.

The invasion will be referred to by the code name *Sealion*.[1]

During the period of preparation and execution of the landings, the armed forces will carry out the following measures:

(a) *Army*. – Will draft a plan for the crossing and operations of the first wave of the invading force. The necessary anti-aircraft batteries will remain under the command of the individual army units until such time as their tasks can be divided into the following groups: support and protection of the land troops, protection of the disembarkation ports, and protection after their occupation of air bases. The Army will allocate landing craft to the individual units and determine, in conjunction with the Navy, the points at which the embarkation and the landings will take place.

(b) *Navy*. – Will provide and safeguard the invasion fleet and direct it to the individual points of embarkation. As far as possible, ships belonging to defeated nations are to be used.

Together with aircraft patrols, the Navy will provide adequate protection on both flanks during the entire Channel crossing. An order on the allocation of commands during the crossing will follow in due course. The Navy will further supervise the establishment of coastal batteries, and will be responsible for the organization of all coastal guns.

The largest possible number of heavy guns must be installed as soon as possible to safeguard the crossing

---

[1] *Seelöwe*.

and to cover both flanks against enemy interference from the sea. For this purpose, anti-aircraft guns mounted on railway bogies (supplemented by all available captured guns) with railway turntables will be used. The Todt Organization will be entrusted with the technical side of the organization.

(c) *Air Force.* – Will prevent all enemy air attacks, and will destroy coastal defences covering the landing points, break the initial resistance of the enemy land forces, and annihilate reserves behind the front. The accomplishment of these tasks will require the closest co-operation between all individual units of the Air Force and the invading Army units. In addition, roads used for troop movements will be attacked and approaching enemy naval vessels engaged before they can reach the embarkation and landing points.

I invite suggestions concerning the use of parachute and airborne troops, and in particular as to whether it would be advisable to keep the parachute and airborne troops in reserve for use only in case of necessity.

¶ 4. The necessary preparations for the installation of signals communications between France and England are being undertaken by the Signals Corps. The armoured under-sea cables are to be laid in co-operation with the Navy.

¶ 5. I hereby order the Commanders-in-Chief to provide me with the following information:

(a) The plans drawn up by the Navy and Air Force for providing the above basic conditions necessary for the Channel crossing (see 2).

(b) A detailed survey of the location of the naval coastal batteries.

(c) An estimate of the shipping space necessary and of the methods of preparation and equipment. Will civilian authorities be asked to co-operate? (*Navy.*)

(d) The organization of air defence in the areas in which the invading troops and vehicles are concentrated. (*Air Force.*)

(*e*) The plan for the Army crossing and operations; the organization and equipment of the first wave.

(*f*) Details of the measures planned by the Navy and Air Force for the execution of the crossing itself, its protection, and the support of the landing operations.

(*g*) Suggestions concerning the use of parachute and airborne troops, and the organization of the anti-aircraft artillery, once the spearhead troops have advanced sufficiently on English soil to permit their use. (*Air Force.*)

(*h*) Location of Army and Naval Headquarters.

(*i*) Are the Army, Navy and Air Force Commanders of the opinion that the invasion should be preceded by a preliminary small-scale landing?

(*signed*) HITLER
(*initialled*) KEITEL
JODL

To these plans there were to be, in the course of the next six weeks, many modifications and elaborations; the idea of the preliminary small-scale invasion was abandoned, so was the unnecessary move to new headquarters; within a week of the issuing of the Directive the date of the invasion was deferred to mid-September. In the main, however, and in most of the details it was to these orders and suggestions that the German Army and Navy – and to a lesser degree the Luftwaffe – diligently applied themselves; this was the great project which they developed, whose preparations they successfully completed, and whose first stage they set in motion at the appointed time.

Why then was the *Sealion* operation not carried out? No doubt of the gravity of the threat; on land and in the air Britain was dangerously weak, Germany demonstrably strong. By September the invasion fleet was ready, the invasion forces organized and equipped. The elimination of Britain as an opponent was of vital importance to Hitler's plans. The moment was favourable, delay might be fatal. What were the reasons for which the expedition was held up, postponed, and eventually cancelled? What overriding influence doomed it to failure?

[1]

The Army Waits

In NORTH-EASTERN France, with the signing of the armistice, the westward flow of refugees had to a large extent been reversed. Horse-drawn farm carts piled high with furniture, flanked by straggling files of men, women and children, plodded back along the melancholy roads beside which the farms stood abandoned and the battered towns were half deserted. On the railways there was little movement other than of German military traffic; the ports were smashed and silent; trade was at a standstill.

With demobilization ordered by the Pétain Government, however, a steady stream of men from such remnants of the French Army as had escaped capture was added to the flow of refugees; men returning to their homes to save something from the wreckage and to garner the harvest. And the people had to live; shops had to supply their needs, markets to serve the countryside and the towns. Cafés and restaurants reopened and gave though grudgingly, comfort to the conquerors. In a little while life resumed something dismally resembling its normal course.

With so large a proportion of the male population captive in Germany there was work for all, and soon an inevitable consequence of occupation had to be faced, a question answered: whether or not to work for the Germans. For some, an unhappy decision to make; yet the enemy was very 'correct' and he paid handsomely; it was perhaps better to do as he asked so as not to be suspected of defiance, risk arrest and deportation. For the Communists – of whom there were large numbers among the industrial workers of the north – it was easy; already before the conquest they had received the Party's orders, issued by Moscow, to collaborate with the enemies of France. So that it was not very long before a numerous labour force became available, without which the Germans could scarcely have accomplished their design.

The calls upon this labour force were many and varied: repair work on the roads, railways and inland waterways, unloading of military stores in railway sidings, and much digging and levelling. Many of the stores were for aircraft, spares and the like; and the levelling was of runways, extending old ones, clearing the ground for new. And, increasingly as time went on, there were heavy bombs to be lifted in the freight yards, hundreds upon hundreds of them; so that long before the Luftwaffe squadrons flew in to land upon the new runways the French were aware of what was afoot.

The enemy made little attempt to hide his purpose. His troops, strictly disciplined, always behaving 'correctly' so as to drive home the propaganda-point that between Germans and Frenchmen there was no cause for enmity, were in the best of good spirits and, off duty, communicative and friendly. They had won an unparalleled victory and they knew it; with morale at the highest point it was ever to reach, they did not trouble to conceal their confident expectation of the next victorious campaign. *'Wir fahren gegen Engel-land!'* they would sometimes sing out. France had been easy, England would be easier. The *Engländer* might be stubborn fighters, but now they were at their last gasp, defeated, without arms.

Towards the end of July the increasing number of enemy troops in the north-east could not fail to be noticed. Fresh formations moved into the towns and spread out over the land, to be billeted in villages and farms or to take over the hotels and villas in the deserted coastal resorts. Troops rolled past in lorries or trudged by singing full-throated military choruses, harsh, incomprehensible. Artillery rumbled over the pavé, heavy guns heavily camouflaged slid by on railway trucks to be shunted into sidings behind the cliffs and headlands of the Pas de Calais. Aircraft – swift fighters, dark twin-engined bombers, stocky dive-bombers – landed on the new airfields. Civilian movement in coastal areas was severely restricted.

Nothing in all this surprised the French. Their senses dulled by disaster it was no more than they, than all France, had come to expect since first the enemy waves had flooded irresistibly over the land. Even whilst the French forces floundered back from river to river the rumour had flown through the country from Paris to the Spanish frontier to bring, in the hour of defeat, both added despair and a measure of consolation. The rumour, amounting to a circumstantial report, that England too would be invaded and conquered, that Göring had told someone in confidence that he would be in London on August 13th and, colourful detail, that on the 15th Hitler would review his victorious troops from Buckingham Palace. Long before the armistice the rumour was accepted and believed, even in the Army, even by staff officers at French Headquarters. Small wonder that the unhappy people of north-eastern France saw nothing strange in the steadily accumulating evidence of things to come.

Here and there as July merged into August details of significant activity were noted. There was renewed movement in the ports, urgent repair work at the docks and quaysides. Along the inland waterways the barges were moving again, almost as in peace-time, but now all in one direction; down the Seine and the Somme, along the canalized Lys and Escaut, some into Belgium, all towards the coast. . . . In the once flourishing summer resorts the remaining inhabitants saw from day to day the German troops, usually in about company strength, assemble on the beaches and march down to the water's edge to stare at the sea as though they had never seen it before. Sometimes the men would embark in small vessels, potter around a short distance from the coast, put in again and scramble out to wade knee-deep to the shore; and then the whole company would face about and shuffle back over the sands, rifles at the ready as if to attack an imaginary enemy lying in the dunes. . . . But speculation about such things was dangerous, curiosity might lead to a charge of spying. The French kept their eyes to the ground and got the belated harvest in.

One thing brought their heads up, during August, with a regularity interrupted only by spells of bad weather: the drone of aircraft engines. A drone that grew to a roar as the machines gained height, joined in formation and swept northward over the coast, out to sea towards England – a brief journey with, it seemed, nothing to bar the way. . . . Nothing? More often than not a change would be noticeable when the machines returned. There were fewer aircraft, in smaller and less regular groups; and some trailed smoke from a damaged engine, others dangled a wheel like the leg of a wounded duck, and more than one crashed before reaching the runway. Day after day the same things happened; signs, unmistakable, that the enemy was not having it all his own way.

The Germans too saw the signs, but without surprise. This was war and losses were inevitable. The Luftwaffe was breaking down the enemy's defences, dispersing his air forces, softening resistance. They had seen it all before, in Poland and Norway, at Sedan and Rotterdam; it was the necessary prelude to easy conquest. 'Give us ten days' fine weather', Göbbels had broadcast, 'and England is finished.' Now, after a poor August, they had the fine weather and not much longer to wait.

Throughout Army Group B, designated to lead the assault, all was now ready. The plans had been completed almost to the last detail; the maps of England and the intelligence handbooks had been distributed to the appropriate sections; the operational schedules had been issued on September 3rd. The military administration of the soon-to-be-conquered country had been laid down, with notices to the civilian population printed in English; the Commander-in-Chief of the Army, Field-Marshal Walther von Brauchitsch, had the documents before him and was about to sign (September 9th) the Quartermaster General's order for the deportation from Britain to the Continent of 'all males between the ages of 17 and 45'. With the organization as nearly perfect as efficient staff work could make it only the word Go from the Supreme Command was needed; the Führer's word signifying that the Luftwaffe had completed its task and that the Navy was ready to put the troops across the Channel. Accustomed to Hitler's last-minute decisions, the Army staff could but hope that he would name the day soon – the day of *Operation Sealion*: S-Day – for of the ultimate result they were confident enough.

The weather remained fine during the first week of September and to the staff at Army headquarters in Fontainbleau it became evident that Göring was reaching towards the objective Hitler had set him: the destruction of the enemy's air defences. What the Luftwaffe did or how it did it was not their immediate concern, but from the reports of the air staff it seemed plain that the battle was going well; the resistance of the Royal Air Force, losing far more fighters than it could afford, was steadily weakening. Presently the stage would be set for the last act, when the Luftwaffe acting as the Army's artillery would blast the English coast defences and, immobilizing the divisions in rear, prepare the way for the invading troops. 'There, on one last island, sits the enemy', Hitler had declared; and of that enemy the German divisions would make short work. Even the commander of Army Group B, the thoughtful and restrained von Rundstedt, on whose shoulders rested full responsibility for the execution of the land campaign, was soberly confident of victory. The British, he well knew, were dogged fighters, but in training and mobility they were no match for their adversaries. 'Once we can gain a foothold on the enemy coast and are advancing inland', he had stated on August 23rd, 'our superiority will show itself clearly.'

The Channel crossing was the Navy's business; it was up to the naval staff to see that business properly conducted and to make sure the flanks were protected as laid down in the Führer's Directive. The Army had heard quite enough of the dangers and difficulties to be aware that in some respects the venture was hazardous; so were all great military undertakings; so had been the Norway expedition, and yet it had led to easy victory in a matter of days. The crossing to England could scarcely be a pleasure cruise, no one expected that; and doubtless the problems of navigation at night, of which the Navy talked so much, would lead to some confusion on the beaches, but it would be nothing with which the initiative of experienced leaders could not deal. As for embarkation and disembarkation, the Army specialists had had plenty of practice crossing the rivers of Belgium and France and some recent training with motor-boats and barges at the mouth of the Ems. Let the Navy put the troops ashore and the Army would know what to do; a few days to build up strength, a week at the most – then forward. With the scattered British divisions in front of them paralysed by the Luftwaffe, on to Portsmouth in the west, to Gravesend in the east, to the Thames valley in the north; to the encirclement of London; to the speedy conquest of England, and '*morgen die ganze Welt*' as the Nazi slogan had it. 'Tomorrow the whole world!'

The transports were coming into the Channel ports, the barges assembling in the inner harbours. Now that they could be seen, examined in detail, the whole operation took on a more exciting reality. Staff officers paid hurried visits, checked capacity and the easy handling of supplies; detachments marched to the quaysides, practice embarkations were timed. More ships were due, many more before the whole fleet was assembled, but the day for launching the operation was drawing near. The Führer had set the provisional date in a secret order; more than that, on September 4th, he had disclosed his firm intention to the Reich and to the world: 'And if they get rather inquisitive over there and ask: "Well then, why doesn't he come?" Rest assured, he is coming!'

The assault troops waited impatiently for the airmen to finish their job. An end must be put to the nightly anxiety and disturbance caused by enemy coastal bombing; from the homeland, from men returning off leave, came reports of air raids on German ports and dockyards – even on Berlin! Little harm was being done, but these last feeble kicks of a defeated enemy were very alarming to wives and families. The Luftwaffe must act promptly now that the Führer had ordered reprisals; for every kilogram of bombs on Germany a thousand kilograms on England whose cities would be erased from the map: '*Wir werden ihre Städte ausradieren!*'

Ready and resolute, with but few qualms, the Army waited for the other two services to complete their tasks. Waited for the preliminary warning from the Führer whom the generals had, not so long ago, regarded as reckless to the point of folly, against whom they had, within the past year, secretly plotted and in whom, since victory in the west, they must tacitly place their trust.

September 6th: S-Day minus 15. From the sea came a sound of gunfire.

[2]

The Führer Reflects

HITLER TOO WAS waiting, with discernible impatience, for Göring's report that air mastery over south-eastern England had at length been gained. That it was about to be gained appeared certain, but the day was fast approaching when, with the need to give the Navy ten day's advance warning, *Sealion's* sailing-date must finally be fixed; time was running short.

This, he was convinced, and Göring agreed, was the moment for the maximum air assault, when the enemy's resistance was diminishing by day and was negligible at night; the moment for the mass attack on London, of whose decisive results he was convinced. The defence of the capital would use up the last of the enemy fighter aircraft, thereby facilitating the destruction of supply centres and other military objectives; and thereafter the bombing of communications, the flight of the populace and the breakdown of administration would exclude the possibility of organized resistance on land. The day of surrender would be brought near, might coincide with or even precede the Day of *Sealion*.

Elsewhere in the watchful world, and not least in the threatened capital, many at that time would have subscribed to his conviction that in the air onslaught upon inland Britain lay the key to conquest. A major error, it was not the one of which he was later to be accused by contemporary historians, who were to blame him not so much for concentrating upon the battles over Kent and Sussex as for his vacillation towards Britain in June and July and the consequent delay in planning *Sealion*. For brief hesitation, however, there were sound reasons; and it is open to doubt whether a greater man in his place would, or could, have moved more swiftly.

To some extent his actions in the summer of 1940 are perhaps more easily understood in the light of his early career, the

formative period of the First World War. Then for the better
part of four years he had, in common with millions of other
unknown men, faced danger and endured boredom behind the
seemingly inexpugnable trench-barrier of the western front and
had pondered the causes of disastrous stalemate. He too had
dreamed of the road to victory, of schemes for going round or
through or over the barrier; schemes that in the minds of their
begetters always had the same glorious termination: the break-
through, sudden and complete, and the annihilation of the
enemy's forces; then the army sweeping along behind the
cavalry, into the enemy's territory, into his capital. And that
was the end. Paris for the Germans, Berlin for the Allies; every
soldier in France, facing east or facing west, had conjured up
that same magnificent vision; on each side men believed that it
would be final, decisive. Seen from the German side, however,
there was one thing wrong with the dream. The capture of
Paris would not have brought about – in 1914 any more than
in 1940 – the end of war with Britain.

This fact Hitler and the great majority of his military
advisers failed to appreciate. The lessons of history, the strength
of Britain's world-wide economy based upon sea power, even
the character of the British people, were neglected or mis-
understood. 'As England, in spite of *the hopelessness of her military
position*, has so far shown herself unwilling to come to any
compromise' – so ran the preamble to the *Sealion* Directive, and
it gave the measure of the Führer's delusion. The war in the
west had not been brought to a victorious conclusion, as he
believed it had, with the fall of France; for England it was only
just beginning. The three-linked chain of sea power – Production, Shipping, Markets – upon which, beneath the shield of the
Navy, depended Britain's continued existence and ability to
wage war, had not yet been seriously damaged or even strained.
Hitler had dipped into Clausewitz; he should have studied
Mahan.

After 1914 many a German soldier had sought an answer to
the distracting question: Why had the Schlieffen plan failed?
Simple: Because the German right hook had not swung wide

enough nor with sufficient strength. To one as unprincipled as Hitler the remedy was easy: Holland next time, as well as Belgium. 'Breach of the neutrality of Belgium and Holland is meaningless', he had declared to his generals on November 23rd, 1939. 'No one will question that when we have won.' So: the Low Countries and the Channel ports 'to get bases', his operational plan stated, 'from which to wage intensive air and sea war against England'.

When after many delays opportunity beckoned in the spring of 1940, General von Manstein suggested a modification to the plan, a shifting of armour from the extreme right to the centre, which immediately appealed to Hitler's intuitive boldness. On May 10th, striking his hardest blow at the weakest point of the French line, he drove through the 'impassable' Ardennes, punched a hole at Sedan, swung right and, thrusting past Arras, reached the coast of Abbeville on the 20th. Small wonder that he jumped for joy. In ten days he had done what the Kaiser's Army had failed to do in four years.

It seemed at first too good to be true. The Army Chief of Staff, General Halder, wrote in his diary on May 17th: 'Führer terribly nervous. Frightened by his own success. . . .' Half encircled to the north-west, the French and British armies were falling back to the sea at Calais and Dunkirk. A tempting prize, but anxiety held him back. On the 18th Halder noted: 'Führer keeps worrying about south flank. He rages and screams that we are on the way to ruin the whole campaign. He won't have any part in continuing the operation in a westward direction.' But it was soon apparent that to the south-west the very heart of France was laid bare and, mastering his fears, he struck straight at it, smashed the dwindling French resistance, hastened on from river to river, and broke and captured the greater part of the French Army. On June 14th German troops entered Paris, and within three days the French Government in Bordeaux begged for mercy. The dream had come true.

According to the precedents of German land strategy, the only ones of which he had any knowledge, he felt entitled to declare: 'The war in the west is ended.' And his subsequent words and actions seem clearly to define his thoughts. He had won the game; his opponent had conceded defeat. He had the right, as Ciano put it, to collect his winnings and get up from the table. Surely the equally defeated partner would not choose to continue alone; surely England, so unprepared for total war and with so much to lose from it, would not dare to challenge the might of victorious Germany. In all probability a 'compromise' could be effected with the help of that political cunning and double-dealing of which he was unquestionably a great master, with crafty peace-feelers put out in neutral capitals during an interval for subversive propaganda in which lurid threats might be blended with common-sense appeals to reason. And in a week or two it might well happen than an encouraging answer would be secretly conveyed through Sweden, Switzerland or Spain, that presently a meeting would be arranged and that once again the 'little worms' would come wriggling to him with their black hats and rolled umbrellas, to negotiate another piece of paper as worthless as the one Chamberlain had taken back from Munich, leaving him free to bend Europe to his will with England a disarmed and sub-servient spectator. He was not alone in thinking that a compromise peace might be acceptable to Britain; half the world thought so too.

That it quickly became apparent that, although one head of the Franco-British alliance had been lopped off, the other was still very much alive and fulminating defiance, only shortened the hopeful interlude of diplomatic intrigue; even while the attempted peace manoeuvres were being stepped up the likely necessity for military action was not neglected. True, Hitler took what amounted to a brief holiday by moving his head-quarters, shortly after the signing of the armistice, from France back to near Freudenstadt in the Black Forest. A period of recuperation was probably essential; after the manifold pre-occupations of the past ten months, the concentrated planning and campaigning of the past three and the emotional nerve-strain of the whirlwind battle of France he needed a rest as much as did the armed forces. But if the tempo was slowed, the consideration of future plans was not interrupted.

For a few days, living a simple life in the quiet Forest, he seems to have been almost contented. Megalomania had not yet conquered all his thoughts, though it had gained the upper hand; he had not yet cut himself off entirely from the communion of other men. He had taken with him, apart from a reduced military staff, two comrades of the first war, and together they motored through the now peaceful countryside of occupied France and Alsace-Lorraine, revisiting the old battlefields. At the end of the month he paid his first visit to Paris, tourist and conqueror; stayed only long enough to see the sights, and returned to the Forest for the first week of July.

For the time being he had good cause for self-satisfaction. Whatever happened, history would remember him for the events of this spring and summer; he had outrivalled those others, the great men of the great German General Staff – Moltke, Falkenhayn, Ludendorff and old Hindenburg. In five weeks he had reached the stature of the proudest military commanders of the past; he the frustrated painter, the battalion runner promoted corporal, the bedraggled revolutionary, the good-for-nothing outcast; in solitary glory beneath the gilded dome of the Invalides he had meditated above Napoleon's tomb. Fate and his own undoubted talents had flattered him dangerously; he could no longer see that in the affairs of men the tide must also ebb. Across the conquered lands his secret police and murder squads stamped their merciless way, sealing his victory with infamy; in the flick of summer sunshine between the pines Hitler was happy.

He might have been entirely contented but for one thing. As time went on he was astonished to discover that England was rejecting his crafty peace overtures. His surprise was genuine; after all he was not begging favours, he was the victor; the British Army had been routed, thrown out of Europe. The English were a sensible Germanic people who must surely see that, despite a warmongering Government and a powerful clique of international Jews, it was necessary to come to terms. England could do nothing against him, whereas he could annihilate England in a month if he chose. . . . However, in the past nothing had been lost by a little waiting. England might yet come to her senses; he must wait until he was quite sure of her attitude.

And meanwhile – Russia? Sooner or later the Communists would have to be smashed. He had assured his Generals that he would not attack in the East before he had dealt with the West; but, with England helpless, he was tempted to try it that autumn – until the Supreme Command staff deferentially pointed out that time was too short to mount so vast an operation, let alone conquer the country, before the coming of winter. It would be best, he conceded to Keitel, to wait till the following spring; by then plans could have been more carefully laid and the fate of England finally settled. He made no final decision, but he agreed in principle: England must come first, compromise or conquest. On July 7th he returned to Berlin.

The Supreme Command staff had not been idle during the Black Forest interlude. The possibility that England would refuse to negotiate had been taken into account. Some delay was unavoidable, very little of it unnecessary. The time-table proves it.

On May 21st – with the Abbeville spearhead moving northward to Boulogne – the Commander-in-Chief of the German Navy, Grand-Admiral Räder, came to see the Führer in his headquarters at Münstereifel and, disclosing in private conversation a tentative naval plan, raised the question of an eventual invasion of England. Hitler would not hear of it. He was in a highly emotional state, overjoyed at early successes, fearful of failure in a campaign he had initiated against the the advice of Brauchitsch; nothing could be allowed to divert strength or attention from the battle in France. Moreover, as he confided to Rundstedt a little later, if France fell, then in his view England would be only too ready to accept an easy peace in which no demands would be made save for the return of ex-German colonies. Räder's question remained unanswered.

It was some time before he could raise it again. The German Command was wholly occupied with the annihilation of the enemy and with the capture of the supreme objective, Paris; it had given no earlier consideration to any invasion problem, it had no time for it now. The Luftwaffe, on the other hand, was fully extended; there were neither transport aircraft nor gliders to spare, and few paratroops available. For naval operations the Channel ports were either devastated, blocked or mined; no ships could be assembled in them for weeks to come. After Dunkirk, when the people of Britain expected it most, invasion as an immediate possibility was out of the question.

On June 20th – the day before the theatrical re-enactment at Compiegne of the signing of the 1918 armistice – Räder again reported to Hitler; first, negatively, on a proposal to occupy Iceland which would have required more warships than the German Navy possessed; secondly, on certain preliminary invasion preparations, for which he proposed the construction of special landing-craft and mentioned minelaying and shipping problems. Hitler, overawed by the unexpected magnitude of his victory, was more interested just then in garnering the fruits of conquest. He committed himself no more than to say, in answer to Räder's suggestion that British naval bases should be bombed forthwith so as to destroy ships under construction or repair, that he was contemplating taking this action in the near future. But his Chief of the Armed Forces Command, Keitel, and his Director of Operations, Jodl, both of whom were present at the meeting, began immediately afterwards to examine the whole question of invasion about which there had recently been signs of awakening interest in Army staff circles. Within twelve days – a relatively short period considering that it covered the signing of the armistice, the move to the Black Forest and Hitler's visit to Paris – they had drawn up a general directive requesting from each of the three services an outline of plans for action against England.

On July 2nd this top secret document was distributed by Keitel. It announced the Führer's decision that a landing in England was to be regarded as a possibility, that the date was still undecided, but that all preliminary preparations were to be begun at once. Working with the utmost speed, the staffs of the three service Commanders-in-Chief – von Brauchitsch,

Göring, Räder – produced in less than a week the information and draft plans required.

In some directions the speed was excessive. On July 10th a Supreme Command order signed by Keitel in the Führer's name commanded preparations to be made for 'strong frontal and flank artillery' to protect the transport and landing of troops 'from the coastal strip Calais – Cap Gris Nez – Boulogne'. Alarmed at the swiftly growing enthusiam of both the Supreme Command and Army staffs, Räder requested an interview with Hitler on the 11th and, fortified by the opinions of the naval staff, voiced his reasoned objections to the whole idea of a large-scale seaborne invasion – planned at short notice and carried out against probably strong enemy opposition – save as a last resort. 'I am convinced', he told the Führer, 'that Britain can be made to ask for peace simply . . . by means of submarine warfare, air attacks on convoys, and heavy air attacks on her main centres. . . . I cannot . . . therefore advocate an invasion of Britain as I did in the case of Norway.'

At hearing the Führer express general agreement with these bold views Räder may have thought himself lucky; unfortunately the agreement was only verbal and, as so often happened with Hitler, meant nothing once the conference was over. Submarine warfare was too slow for Hitler's purpose; the Army's invasion plan coupled with Luftwaffe bombing was more to his liking. He continued drafting the new Directive.

On the 15th the naval staff received from the Supreme Command a telephone warning of the probable contents of Directive 16, and on the next day it was distributed: *'Preparations for the Invasion of England.'* The operation to be ready for launching by the middle of August.

Thus: April 10th – Oslo. May 15th – Holland. June 14th – Paris. July 16th – *Sealion* Directive. August 15th (provisionally) – England, capitulation or conquest. Four months from start to finish. From British ridicule – 'Hitler has missed the bus' – to Britain's downfall: 'if necessary the island will be occupied'. It was speedy enough.

Subsequent delays were not directly attributable to Hitler.

Given the scale of the operation, given also that no previous preparations had been made, it was inevitable that the building up of a suitable invasion force should take more time than the brief period allowed by the Directive. Provision of sea transport apart, the assault troops had to be trained and equipped, detailed adjustments made to Army plans, inter-service arguments thrashed out and settled by the Supreme Command; the redeployment of the Luftwaffe could not be achieved in the twinkling of an eye, and the initial air attack was held up by bad weather. In none of these matters was Hitler's attitude obstructive or even vacillating. He still hoped to totter British morale before striking a blow, but the expectation of easy 'compromise' was past. Angrily disappointed at England's recalcitrance, he wanted to finish the job quickly – by sea, from the air, by means of subversive propaganda and grisly threats, or by a combination of all three – it mattered little how. 'Rest assured, he is coming!' A bogeyman menace, it was no bluff. Britain must, and would, submit to his will.

Late in August the bombing of Berlin had both increased his impatience and provided him with a sound reason for advancing the date of the prelude to total victory. A blow to German prestige, after Göring's rash assurance of invulnerability, the bombing also supplied the essential pretext for the devastation of London; and the rage of his speech of September 4th – as usual so well contrived that it infected his hearers – stimulated his people to much anticipatory gloating at the prospect of England's forthcoming destruction. At 'we shall rub their cities out' he was cheered hysterically by a vast audience consisting largely of women and social workers.

As the first week in September drew to its close, and the Army stood ready and the ships began to assemble in the invasion ports, he waited fretfully for the final phase. Only one thing, as he saw it, could stop him now: the English weather. Rain and low cloud that might delay the work of the airmen over England, storms that might hold up the transports in the Channel. With confidence in the strength of his position, in the might of his armed forces and in the results of aerial bombardment, it was his only serious doubt. Were strong winds and high seas to hinder the sailing of *Sealion* until the end of the month, it might be wise, even advantageous, to let the Luftwaffe complete the subjugation of England and to postpone the invasion until after the enemy had surrendered, perhaps until the spring. Not all the seed sown by Räder had fallen upon stony ground.

[3]

The Grand-Admiral's Dilemma

THE STRONG ARGUMENT against invasion in 1940, developed by Räder in conference with Hitler on July 11th, was the logical outcome of ten months of maritime warfare. But the premise of the argument went even farther back than that and had been stated by Räder, in a confidential report to his staff, on September 3rd, 1939: 'Today, the war against England and France broke out, the war which, according to the Führer's previous assertion, we had no need to expect before about 1944.' Point one: the war had come five years too soon.

Had Hitler possessed sufficient patience to postpone his planned war until the promised five years had elapsed, the German Navy, by virtue of its authorized building programme, would certainly have grown to formidable strength. That Britain, alive to the peril since Munich, would have countered by rebuilding and increasing her own Navy is not to be doubted, and her shipyards were better equipped to do so than those of Germany; yet, as Räder put it, 'the prospect of defeating the British Fleet and cutting off supplies, in other words of settling the British question conclusively, would have been good'. Hitler's impetuous bad faith had averted that danger for Britain.

For Räder it was therefore with grave misgivings that he had confronted the premature opening of the war at sea. Initially as defeatist as the Army leaders, his view was that his surface vessels could 'do no more than show that they know how to die gallantly'. Only by the patient use of his few U-boats could he hope to inflict lasting damage, but even so he had to admit that 'the submarine arm is still much too weak to have any decisive effect'.

Nor could the pocket battleships, of which only two were immediately operational, 'be decisive for the outcome of the war'. Worse still, the activities of both submarines and battleships were restricted by Hitler in the hope that France and Britain would be lulled by a false sense of security until after the conquest of Poland.

It was not long before his anxiety was increased. Hardly had the Polish campaign been brought to its inevitable end than Hitler set his military staff to the planning of *Operation Yellow*, the campaign against the Low Countries and France to be launched that autumn. For the German Navy the role allotted would evidently be minor, but in what must surely follow the success of *Yellow* it could only be major. Already in November 1937 Hitler had declared his aggressive intentions to the three Commanders-in-Chief: first Austria, Czechoslovakia, Poland, and then in swift succession France and that 'hateful enemy' England. Despite the Führer's firm belief that Britain would come to terms rather than fight alone, Räder was early convinced that sooner or later the final operation – granted success in the others – must mean invasion. And he saw the danger.

The danger was that the relatively weak German Navy would be diverted from its only valid purpose, that of attacking British supply routes in a war bound to be long, to concentration upon a single enterprise in which all would be hazarded upon a gambler's throw. Forewarned by the preparations for *Yellow*, he forearmed himself by putting the naval staff to work drawing up their own plans for the invasion of England. More a list of prerequisites than a detailed study, the plans specified as a first essential for landings limited to Kent and Sussex the possession of the Continental Channel ports and coastline – in November 1939 still well beyond the German grasp. Although the Army was consulted, the plans were not disclosed to Hitler; secretly filed, they were held in reserve as a measure of self-protection against any sudden demand for major offensive action. No other preparations were made, no action was taken.

When, thereafter, *Operation Yellow* was several times postponed, eventually until the spring, Räder and his Chief of Staff, Admiral Schniewind, may well have thought themselves lucky not to have been driven to a vain sacrifice of the fleet before new ships were completed and additional submarines came from the yards; the war of attrition against British warships and supply routes could now continue and slowly gather momentum. And yet it was not long before the Grand-Admiral began to develop other and more grandiose plans of his own devising; schemes to put into effect an operation which, making full use of the German fleet to achieve a result out of all proportion to its strength, would at one and the same time safeguard the vital interests of his own country, strike a wounding blow at British sea power and, outbidding the bombastic Göring and the Luftwaffe, enhance his prestige and that of his service in the eyes of the Führer.

Norway! Before the year was out he and Schniewind, without waiting for the doubting Führer's unqualified approval, had renounced the clean sea air of naval affairs to enter the dark and fetid alleyways of plots and perfidy arm-in-arm with the traitor Quisling. No doubt there were cogent reasons of State to urge them on. The Scandinavian iron ore was vital to Germany at war, supplying no less than 11,000,000 tons of the 15,000,000 required annually; and, of this eleven million, throughout the long northern winter four and a half came by sea down the Norwegian coast from Narvik and Kirkenes. Norway was neutral, but Anglo-Norwegian amity drawing ever closer seemed to menace that neutrality, to threaten the cutting of the iron ore supply-line. 'It must be made impossible for Norway to fall into British hands', Räder told Hitler, 'as this would be decisive for the outcome of the war.'

Early in the New Year his anxiety was further heightened. Incidents increased, so did the hostility of the Norwegian people. The Russo-Finnish war was tempting an Allied expedition to the aid of the Finns; the occupation of Norway seemed to be a likely result. In February the *Altmark* affair, in which captive British merchant seamen were released by the intervention of the destroyer *Cossack* in Norwegian territorial waters, strengthened Räder's intention and alarmed the Führer. The plot became a plan, the plan an operation: *Weserübung* ('Exercise Weser').

In its Directive, Hitler stated: 'On principle we will do our utmost to make the operation appear as a peaceful occupation. . . . It is most important that the Scandinavian States as well as the Western opponents should be taken by surprise by our measures.'

To this Räder replied, in conference on March 9th: 'Operation *Weserübung* is urgent. The C.-in-C. Navy feels it his duty, however, to present to the Führer a clear picture regarding the character of the naval operation. . . . The operation in itself is contrary to all principles in the theory of naval warfare. According to this theory, it could be carried out by us only if we had naval supremacy. We do not have this; on the contrary, we are carrying out the operation in face of the vastly superior British fleet. In spite of this the C.-in-C. Navy believes that, provided surprise is complete, our troops can and will successfully be transported to Norway.'

And so, on April 9th, they were. Although the treacherous surprise was not complete, so successful was the operation as a whole that already on the 10th Räder, after reporting to Hitler, was able to note: 'At the beginning and at the conclusion of the conference the Führer expressed his full appreciation to the C.-in-C. Navy for the great achievement of the Navy.'

The gain to Germany was immense. In the course of a few weeks the entire Allied maritime situation in northern waters had been transformed. For Britain, instead of a friendly neutral across the North Sea limiting the area of naval patrol, there was now a hostile coastline dominated by the long-ranging bombers of the Luftwaffe; the tenuous patrol-line had been thrown back to the island-chain – Orkneys, Shetlands, Faroes, Iceland – leading to the Denmark Strait and the icebound Greenland shore. At one stroke Germany had secured the vital iron-ore route, had all but broken the stranglehold of naval blockade, and had gained for her armed forces what Hitler called 'a wider start-line against Britain'. Well might Räder find satisfaction at the result of his nefarious plotting.

Of that plotting against the Government of a friendly power it may perhaps be urged in limited extenuation that he had undertaken it in the belief that his country's ability to avert defeat was at stake, since Britain was planning to cut off the iron ore supplies. In any event, his share in Hitler's evil policies apart, he had proved himself to be a strategist of considerable worth, one who understood the business of sea war, the penetrating influence of sea power. Not a winning personality – though, in a land of more liberal traditions, he might have become so – his contemporaries saw him as a stern, unbending disciplinarian whose rare smile was tight lipped and fleeting. Superficially the impression was of haughtiness, so that although he had the welfare of his men at heart he was more respected than popular; in his own service more respected than Hitler.

Drawn into political intrigues between the wars, he had more than once been forced to trim his sails to the wind of official disapproval; but of his keenness and conscientious ability as a naval officer there had never been any doubt. Serving his apprenticeship in the great days of the Kaiser's Navy before 1914, he had skipped the normal stage of commanding a ship at sea to become Chief of Staff to Admiral Hipper, leader of the German battle-cruiser squadrons at the Dogger Bank and Jutland. From Hipper he had learned much; cruiser warfare was his speciality; in temporary retirement in 1922 he had written a sound book upon the subject.

Hitler, unfortunately, he venerated: the leader risen miraculously from the people, the man who had re-established Prussian discipline in a united Germany, who had recreated the Army and the Air Force in defiance of the Versailles Treaty, above all the man who had revived the German Navy and had confirmed him, Erich Räder, as its Commander-in-Chief and promoted him to Grand-Admiral. He admired the man, too, for his frank admission of total ignorance and fear of the sea; the Führer had sought his advice, had listened to his expert counsel on naval matters and sea power generally. It was a source of pride to him: in all Hitler's entourage he alone knew anything of maritime affairs.

For most of the members of that entourage he had little liking. The army leaders for the greater part looked down upon the junior service; they always had. Although in critical times they might expect much from it, their faith was wholly pinned to a time-honoured strategy of which they had absorbed all the lessons of the First World War save that of the pervading influence of sea power. As for Göring, who for purely selfish reasons had obstructed the development of the Navy's air arm – Göring with his 'disastrous influence', his 'unimaginable vanity', his 'dishonesty, ignorance and selfishness . . . an effeminate and unsoldierly character'[1] – for Göring he felt both contempt and a deep hatred based upon fear.

The Reichsmarschall was his senior in rank and stood closer to the Führer in whom he had instilled, with his 'unrestrained ambition', much of his own reckless and arrogant belief in the all-conquering might of the Luftwaffe. In mid-May, as the Wehrmacht smashed its way through the flimsy western barriers and the Channel ports came tumbling into the bag, the fear grew. The fear that Göring, with his 'craving for cheap popularity and effect' and his eye upon the glittering prize of England, might swing Hitler to an impulsive demand for premature naval action in support of the Luftwaffe, action which the Navy would be quite incapable of taking. To forestall Göring was more than wise, it was a duty; but to tackle the Führer in the midst of his campaign could be dangerous.

Räder, however, providing he knew how to play his hand, held several good cards. On May 21st he played the first: proved his foresight by disclosing the Navy's tentative invasion scheme. Hitler made no bid; and Räder, reassured, appreciated the time gained for a revision of naval plans, made essential by losses off Norway. On June 20th he played the second, a slightly stronger card from the same suit; but this time a dual purpose was discernible. First and foremost he wanted to persuade Hitler to force Göring's hand, to get the Luftwaffe to take immediate action against the Royal Navy, now while the golden opportunity offered of catching England off her balance, confused by defeat.

In this, as already noted, he failed. To his calling attention in conference 'to the necessity of starting vigorous air attacks on British bases in order to destroy ships under construction and repair', he drew only: 'The Führer contemplates taking such action soon.' To his 'report on the preparations for an invasion

[1] From Räder's testimony at the Nuremberg trials, quoted by Martienssen in *Hitler and his Admirals*.

of England', there was no forthright reply. The time was not ripe; the Führer had taken Paris by strength, he would take London by stealth. Wait and see.

His second purpose was to finesse a card from the Army, to find out their intentions regarding England. 'The Army must check the composition of the divisions required', he put in as an aside at the conference. And in this purpose he succeeded all too well. The Army, he discovered, had made no plans for invasion, had not even considered it; but now that it was on the cards they showed suddenly an almost dangerous enthusiasm. Within ten days they had so shaped their ideas that Keitel could issue the Supreme Command Directive in which the Führer announced that 'a landing in England is possible' and ordered all preparations 'to be begun immediately'.

With dismay Räder read the instructions for the Navy, requiring information on shipping available 'for strong Army forces (25–40 divisions)', suggesting 'landings on a broad front' and adding that 'the invading forces must be highly mechanized and numerically superior to the opposing armies'. The Army meanwhile was to discover 'the extent to which the British Army will have been re-equipped a month or so hence. . . .' A month or so! – the golden opportunity was to be allowed to slip by whilst a full-scale military plan was slowly mounted; a plan in which, as he had feared, the Navy would be called upon to play a major part. One phrase alone gave hope: 'the invasion is still only a plan, and has not yet been decided upon'. On July 11th, again stressing the need for immediate air attacks, he had played for the first time the card of strong objection to the whole scheme.

In vain. Five days later Directive No. 16 was issued and Räder was shocked to read: 'The landing operations must be a surprise crossing on a broad front extending approximately from Ramsgate to a point west of the Isle of Wight. Units of the Luftwaffe will do the work of artillery and *units of the Navy the work of engineers.*' Shades of Tirpitz! Of the old fork-bearded Grand-Admiral who, at the turn of the century, had planned and developed the High Seas Fleet, only to see his plans stultified by the Kaiser and the General Staff in 1914: 'The

Army', he had written, 'marched into the world war with . . . the natural superiority which it possessed over the Navy in consequence of the prevailing land tradition in Germany; it still looked upon the Fleet as a kind of pioneer detachment of the Army.'

Quarter of a century later the same attitude, almost the same words. And an impossible scheme: 'broad front . . . Ramsgate to the Isle of Wight . . . the Navy to do the work of engineers' – and 40 divisions! But if the words were the Army's, the orders were Hitler's. If Räder obeyed them unquestioningly he would fail; if he refused – if he dared to disobey the Fuhrer! – dismissal, ruin. Dangerous dilemma.

[4]

The Light-Cruiser Squadron

IT IS PROBABLE that in all the circle of advisers about Hitler at this time only Räder fully appreciated the facts of German naval weakness; and, in his dealings with Supreme Headquarters, it was therefore in isolation that he had to face the inexorable logic of those facts. Of the maritime situation as a whole, the Army leaders were entirely ignorant because they had never been taught to concern themselves with it; the Luftwaffe – Göring and his air-fleet commanders Sperrle and Kesselring – were equally ignorant because, over-confident in the value of air power, they were convinced that sea power was unnecessary for the subjugation of Britain. With such unenlightened opinions subordinate commanders and their staffs were in automatic agreement, content to accept Göbbel's phrase that the only important adjunct needed for England's total defeat was ten days' fine weather.

How much Hitler grasped of maritime affairs it is hard to tell. He had been kept informed of all the details, had approved all major decisions, had listened to Räder's periodic reports since the beginning of the war; and yet it seems more than likely that, in his feverish concentration upon vast land adventures and his emotional overjoy at success, naval developments were now eluding his memory. In the naval conferences he spoke easily about other things – about the 'New Order' in his newly-conquered Europe, about the 'Herrenvolk', about the desirability of settling Jews in Madagascar; sometimes about Russia, seldom about the sea. Doubtless he remembered the early successes, the sinkings of the aircraft-carrier *Courageous* and the armed merchant-cruiser *Rawalpindi*, as well as Prien's brilliant exploit in destroying the battleship *Royal Oak* in Scapa Flow; he may have forgotten some of the losses.

Only one event had been spectacular. But what a spectacle! – observed by tens of thousands from the waterfront of

Montevideo. Fortunately for Räder, the self-destruction of the *Graf Spee* as the alternative to fighting her way out had been approved by the Führer. A lamentable episode; from the unhappy start when, after Harwood's skilful surmise at the *Spee's* whereabouts, the three British cruisers had dashed in – 'like destroyers' Langsdorf had said – to the shameful finish when the battleship had turned tail and made for neutral waters. The truth, or the greater part of it, had been kept from the German people, but not from Hitler.

For the sake of German prestige it had perhaps been fortunate that just then world attention had, for a few days, been held by the *Spee* adventure, because on the very night before the River Plate action there had occurred another regrettable incident. In the night of December 11th–12th, 1939, three German light cruisers returning to the Heligoland Bight after covering a minelaying operation off the Tyne had been intercepted by a British submarine – the *Salmon*, it was later reported. Despite the utmost precautions, both the *Nürnberg* and the *Leipzig* had been torpedoed and seriously damaged; only the greatest efforts had enabled the two vessels to reach a home port. The naval staff might be glad to report that the *Nürnberg*, repaired just in time to take part in the Norway campaign, was now back in Kiel; about the *Leipzig*, however, Räder was not so happy. It would be a very long time before she could be made serviceable again, and even then only for training purposes.

After that had come a period of relative immunity, in which but a few torpedo craft and U-boats had been lost, so that taking operations as a whole the balance had not been unfavourable to the German Navy. It had, however, to be admitted that neither the carrier *Ark Royal* nor the battleship *Nelson* had yet been sunk, as Nazi propaganda had so triumphantly proclaimed. As for Norway, the Führer had been warned beforehand of the losses to be expected and had accepted them without demur. Räder could but hope that he would not react too violently if it became necessary to recall them to his memory. They were not inconsiderable; indeed they made all the difference to future plans.

First in importance the *Blücher*, that fine new heavy cruiser of which much had been expected: sunk by the Norwegian land defences in Oslo fiord at dawn on April 9th. Sunk, when by all the rules of chance and of cunning calculation – no warning, no ultimatum, no declaration of war – she should have steamed safely in on her 'peaceful' mission of seizing capital, king and gold reserve. Already during the previous night in the Skagerrak a British submarine – the *Truant*, it later transpired – had got the cruiser *Karlsruhe* as well as one of the troopships. And next morning it had been the turn of the *Königsberg* of the same class; first damaged by the Bergen shore batteries, then sunk by British aircraft – a smack in the eye for Göring that; after all his big talk, the first major warship to be sunk from the air: German! Sunk, moreover, by the Royal Navy's relatively weak Fleet Air Arm, whose *Skua* fighter-bombers had operated at almost incredibly long range from Hatston in the Orkneys. That had been on the 10th, and next day the pocket battleship *Lützow* (ex-*Deutschland*) was torpedoed by the submarine *Spearfish* and so seriously damaged that she was likely to be out of action for a year or more.

Then had occurred that serious setback in the Narvik fiord. Destroyers, supply vessels, a U-boat, an ammunition ship, all lying in apparent safety – annihilated, on two fateful days, April 10th and 13th, by the undeniably daring attack of half a dozen British destroyers assisted, rather unfairly Räder might think, by the 15-inch-gun battleship *Warspite* – she who, with a jammed helm, had steamed two full circles out of control under the German guns at Jutland. A major disaster: ten destroyers lost, ten out of the German Navy's total of nineteen. And now, even allowing for new construction, the total available was down to eight.

Fully as bad, from the point of view of present operations, had been the putting out of commission of the twin battleships[1] *Scharnhorst* and *Gneisenau*. Already on April 9th the *Renown* had seriously damaged the latter; probably the appalling weather conditions alone had saved the German ship from destruction.

---

[1] This was the German classification of these powerful vessels. The British described them as battle-cruisers, given their relatively light armament of nine 11-inch guns and their high speed.

True, the *Scharnhorst* had more than repaid the injury two months later, on June 9th, by sinking the carrier *Glorious* and her attendant destroyers *Ardent* and *Acasta*; but the price of victory had been heavy. The *Acasta*, refusing the chance to escape under cover of smoke, had gallantly attacked and scored a torpedo hit before being overwhelmed by gunfire. From Räder's point of view it was a good thing that, as far as could be ascertained, no survivors had got back to England to tell of the serious damage inflicted on the *Scharnhorst*, damage that would keep her in dry-dock for a clear six months. The same repair period went for the *Gneisenau*: torpedoed ten days later by the submarine *Clyde*. Just as well if confusion between the two ships – and indeed the similarity in outline of all major German

Table 1

NAME	CLASS	CONDITION
Scharnhorst	Battleship	Out of action 6 months from June 1940
Gneisenau	Battleship	Out of action 6 months from June 1940
Graf Spee	Pocket battleship	Scuttled after defeat, December 1939
Lützow	Pocket battleship	Out of action 12 months from April 1940
Blücher	Heavy cruiser	Sunk, April 1940
Karlsruhe	Light cruiser	Sunk, April 1940
Königsberg	Light cruiser	Sunk, April 1940
Leipzig	Light cruiser	Out of action 12 months from December 1939
Heidkamp *Schmidt* *Thiele* *Lüdemann* *Künne* *von Röder* *Zenker* *Giese* *Köllner* *von Arnim*	Destroyers (10)	Sunk, April 1940
—	U-boats (28)	Sunk to end August 1940

warships – should prove puzzling to the British; in all probability some time would pass before they realized that both twin battleships were now out of commission, that in addition the pocket battleship *Admiral Scheer* was undergoing a lengthy refit, and that the heavy cruiser *Hipper* was back in port in none too satisfactory a state: endurance bad, machinery giving trouble, not to mention the considerable damage – a 120-foot-long gash in the bow – done by the last desperate attack of the sinking destroyer *Glowworm* on April 8th.

Together with the U-boat losses, the statement of German warships which would play no part in *Sealion* was not unimpressive (see table 1).

Time was essential for Räder; time to repair and refit, to bring into service some of those great new ships of which Hitler's premature commencement of hostilities had deprived him (see table 2).

Table 2

NAME	CLASS	CONDITION
Bismarck	Battleship	Not operational until March 1941
Tirpitz	Battleship	Not operational until September 1941
Prince Eugen	Heavy cruiser	Not operational until end of 1940
Admiral Scheer	Pocket battleship	Not operational until mid-October (refitting)
Graf Zeppelin	Aircraft carrier	Never completed

There were also the two venerable battleships *Schlesien* and *Schleswig-Holstein*, of pre-1914 and even pre-*Dreadnought* vintage. They had been of some use against the defenceless Poles in the previous September, but they would be worse than sitting ducks if used in connection with *Sealion*. Even for limited duty as bombardment vessels there was now no time to refit and re-equip them.

What, then, was there left? What strength would be available for the German Navy this September to leap the hurdle Napoleon had refused in September 135 years ago? (see table 3).

Table 3

NAME	CLASS	REMARKS
Admiral Hipper	Heavy cruiser	Eight 8-inch. Endurance low, machinery unreliable
Köln[1]	Light cruiser	Nine 5·9-inch
Nürnberg	Light cruiser	Nine 5·9-inch
Emden	Light cruiser	Eight 5·9-inch. Ageing. Damaged off Oslo. Normally used only for training
—	U-boats	26 operational, but less than 12 fit for long-range working
—	Destroyers	8 ready for sea

[1] Damaged by naval aircraft off Norway, but repaired by mid-August.

And that was all, with the addition of between 40 and 50 small torpedo craft and fast motor-boats useful for harassing merchant vessels in narrow waters and fine weather. But it was not all the story of German naval weakness. The price of guarding Norway was naval vigilance; though the Luftwaffe shared the work, the coast required ceaseless watching by sea; British submarines were active, surface raids expected. The Baltic could not be left entirely to the Russians. The Atlantic offered too important an opportunity for damaging attacks to be denuded of U-boats. The *Hipper*, her endurance still too low for successful commerce raiding, might be used to draw off heavy ships from Scapa; but it would be vain then to commit the remaining small force of cruisers and destroyers to the Channel where, against the still powerful British forces in home waters, it would risk annihilation.

To Räder it was clear enough: the German Navy could give no substantial support to a seaborne invasion that summer. Postponement was the answer. But how to convince Hitler of that? And how explain to the Supreme Command and to the Army, who thought invasion 'easy', that after ten months of victorious war the supposedly powerful German fleet was now no more than a weak squadron of light cruisers?

[5]

The Limiting Factor

To say that the German naval staff received the orders contained in Directive No. 16 with dismay would be an understatement. They were clearly horrified. The condescension of the phrase 'the Navy will do the work of engineers' might rankle, it was the naïve amateurishness of the Führer's assumption that shocked them. To imply in an operational order that an opposed crossing of a considerable area – 'from Ramsgate to west of the Isle of Wight' – of a sea whose moods were notoriously unpredictable was no greater a feat than the bridging of a river seemed to reach a dangerous height of military fatuity. That such an opinion must have emanated either from the cold but usually clear-sighted Jodl – the servile Keitel scarcely counted – from the Army Commander-in-Chief Brauchitsch, or his excitable Chief of Staff Halder, did nothing to diminish the peril; Hitler had drafted the Directive and signed the order.

The horns of Räder's dilemma were sharpened. As naval Commander-in-Chief he could not let the order stand unchallenged. As one who had taken the personal oath of obedience to Hitler he could neither refuse duty nor demand the order's cancellation. He must move swiftly, but with caution. After all his careful play, the Army had dealt him an impossible hand; and, avoiding a direct approach to the Führer, it was to the Army he replied.

On July 19th, within three days of the receipt of Directive No. 16, the naval staff presented a memorandum to the staff at Supreme Headquarters. A lengthy document, it opened up such a vista of valid difficulties none of which had been considered or even envisaged by the Supreme Command that Keitel and Jodl – who, swimming with the tide of Army opinion, had both swung round to the view that the planned invasion would be 'quite a simple operation' – had no choice but to pass the memorandum to Hitler.

Two days later, on the 21st, the Führer summoned a conference of Commanders-in-Chief[1] in Berlin and made what, for him, appeared to be an open-minded examination of the entire situation. Britain's defiance still puzzled him; she must, he supposed, be counting on assistance either from America or from Russia and so 'naturally it is our duty to deliberate the American and Russian questions carefully'. The Commanders-in-Chief, however, had little opportunity to deliberate; Hitler did it for them.

'A speedy termination of the war', he declared, 'is in the interest of the German people.' But this, given the present favourable situation, was not urgently necessary: 'an abundance of material is available . . . food supplies are assured for some time. The fuel problem . . . will not become critical as long as Roumania and Russia continue their supplies'. Nevertheless, 'it is necessary to clear up the question of whether a direct operation could bring Britain to her knees'.

To Räder all this must have seemed sweetly reasonable, and his hopes of cancellation or at least postponement of the *Sealion* operation may well have risen as the Führer quoted as his own some of the naval staff's weighty admonitions. 'The invasion of Britain is an exceptionally daring undertaking, because even if the way is short, this is not just a river crossing, but the crossing of a sea which is dominated by the enemy. This is not a case of a single crossing operation as in Norway; operational surprise cannot be expected; a defensively prepared and utterly determined enemy faces us and dominates the sea area which we must use. . . .'

So far so good. The Army was warned; they would have to think twice. The Führer had shown that he understood the naval objections; surely he would modify the orders. He failed to do so; and ended the conference by adhering to the initial demand: 'For the Army operation, 40 divisions will be required.'

After that, for the time being, there was nothing more to be said. No one cared to contradict the Führer, and Räder had to

[1] Only Räder's rough notes are available for this meeting, and in them there is no naming of those present. From several indications, however, the impression is gained that all three services were represented, and from the wording of Hitler's harangue it seems clear that he was not addressing Räder alone.

get on with the job. Although he had recited the many pre-requisites and stressed the possibility of bad weather after mid-September, he had obtained only one concession: 'If it is not certain that preparations can be completed by the beginning of September', Hitler had agreed, 'other plans must be considered.' It was a very small hope. The Army, reporting on the following day (July 22nd) that preparations could not in any event be completed by mid-August, had no doubt whatever of achieving readiness a month later, whilst the Luftwaffe was boisterously convinced that by mid-September England would be *erledigt* – eliminated.

Räder wisely held his hand; set the naval staff to work and, on July 25th, again met Hitler in conference. This time, pointing out the quite exceptional strain which the provision of shipping for the invasion would impose on German economy, he requested absolute priority for the requisitioning of shipping and shipyards in Germany and western Europe. The Führer agreed. Tugs, lighters and small motor vessels had already been earmarked; the work of requisition and modification now started in earnest.

In the memorandum of July 19th the naval staff had not pulled their punches. The phrasing was clear enough for even the most land-minded soldier to understand if he set his mind to it.

'The task allotted to the Navy in *Operation Sealion* is out of all proportion to the Navy's strength and bears no relation to the tasks that are set the Army and the Luftwaffe', was one of its hard-hitting sentences. And there were others equally direct: 'The landing operations on the English coast will find him (the enemy) resolved to throw in fully and decisively all his naval forces.' And again, and most significantly: 'It cannot be assumed that the Luftwaffe alone will succeed in keeping the enemy naval forces clear of our shipping' – to which was added, perhaps as a sop to Göring's vanity; 'as its operations are very dependent on weather conditions.'

In conclusion the memorandum had drawn attention to a consideration that, albeit of paramount importance, had hitherto escaped the notice of the Supreme Command. 'These reflections cause the naval staff to see exceptional difficulties that cannot be assessed individually until a detailed examination of the transport problem has been made.'

The question of transport did not appear to have been examined at all by the Army; or, if it had, it had been brushed aside as being entirely a matter for the Navy 'doing the work of engineers'. Certainly the least reflection or previous consultation with the naval staff would have brought about a sensible modification of the sweeping demand, sanctioned by the Führer, for 40 divisions; for, even if much hard bargaining was bound to ensue between the services before the balance of requirement and availability was fairly established, it was a matter of simple fact – almost of simple arithmetic – to prove that the demand could not be fulfilled.

Long and intricate calculations of shipping space would have to be made before the problems presented by *Sealion* could finally be solved, but no more than a brief estimate by the naval staff was needed to show the absurdity of the initial plan. The Army's suggested first-wave force of some 300,000 men, with supplies, guns, vehicles and equipment, would require something over 2,100,000 tons of shipping; and the short answer to that was that, in all the ports and harbours of Germany, so much tonnage did not exist. Nor, had it existed, could it have been accommodated in the Channel ports; as the naval memorandum had stated: 'harbour installations and adjacent inland water-ways have been extensively damaged through the fighting in the campaign in France, or are of limited capacity'.

As for the causes of this shipping shortage which had now to be faced by the Supreme Command, they were due in the main to the situation that had been foreseen on the day, April 3rd, 1939, when Hitler had ordered the armed forces to prepare for the attack on Poland. The German Navy, issuing its war plans in May, had taken into consideration amongst other important purposes the defence of Germany's sea communications, but Hitler's premature action had compelled the qualification that 'the Navy is faced with a task to which its present development

does not correspond'; and Räder had never concealed from
Hitler that the enemy's maritime power would in due course
inevitably strangle German overseas trade. Believing in a short
war ending, after the swift defeat of Poland, in a negotiated
compromise with France and Britain, Hitler had accepted the
risk. That, as events had turned out, the vast and complicated
machinery of British sea power applied to a distant blockade
had taken time to come into full operation and that the delay
had enabled Germany to recall many of her ships in the early
months of the war, had made but little difference to the
position predicted by Räder and reached by midsummer 1940.
Propaganda had acclaimed such successes as the return of the
great liner *Bremen*; but if the truth were told her safety had been
due less to German skill than to the strict observance of international law – foolish in Nazi eyes – by the British submarine
commander who had intercepted her. For the rest, it was
heartening to know that, in ten months, nearly half a million
tons of shipping had run the gauntlet of the British blockade
and that now, with the whole coastline of Continental Europe
either in the German grip or falling under German control,
still more might be expected to return; yet for the immediate
requirements of an operation on the scale of *Sealion* the shipping
situation remained ineluctably sombre.

Before the war Germany had possessed some 3,500,000 tons
of seagoing shipping.[1] Of this total not far short of 2,000,000
tons had been, in September 1939, on voyage or in ports
beyond the British Isles and the Atlantic coast of France; a
round 1,000,000 tons was employed in the Baltic and Scandinavian trade; and the remainder was engaged either in North
Sea fishing or in the coastal trade from the Baltic to Belgium. A
year later, despite strenuous efforts to get the overseas shipping
home, more than 1,000,000 tons was lying in mostly distant
foreign ports and of the nearly equal amount that had tried to
break the blockade some 350,000 tons had been intercepted and
either captured or scuttled. Allowing for losses from all causes
during and after the Norwegian campaign, there remained in

[1] The term 'seagoing' is used for convenience to include both *ocean* shipping
(about 2,500,000 tons) and *coastal* shipping.

German hands scarcely 2,250,000 tons, of which a considerable proportion was needed both for the vitally important Baltic and Scandinavian trade (including the iron ore traffic and the supply of raw materials from Russia) and for supplying the forces of the occupation in Norway. Relatively little seagoing tonnage had been captured in the Low Countries or in western France and thus, given that passenger liners and other large vessels were quite unsuitable for military operations in the narrow waters of the Channel, all that the naval staff could scrape together for the transporting of the invasion army's essential vehicles, equipment and supplies were some 170 vessels of a total tonnage of roughly 750,000.

Approximately and in round numbers the German shipping situation in September 1940 could therefore be analysed as shown in table 4 (see page 58).[1]

From this it is evident that the amount by which the available shipping fell short of the Army's invasion requirement corresponded almost exactly with the total of tonnage blocked in neutral ports together with that intercepted and captured or scuttled. Admittedly, many of the ships blocked overseas would have been unsuitable for use as invasion transports because of their size (10,000 tons and over), but they would certainly have been suitable for the Baltic whence smaller vessels could then have been released for the cross-Channel expedition. It is therefore true to say that the pressure of sea power was the cause of the deficit. Together with naval weakness, lack of merchant shipping was *Sealion's* limiting factor. The Royal Navy had made it so.

---

[1] The figures have been checked and counter-checked with the help of the following: (i) Lloyd's Lists, (ii) Official Naval History (*The War at Sea*, Vol. 1), (iii) *The Defence of the U.K. 1939–45* (Official War History Series), (iv) *The Economic Blockade of Germany* (Official War History Series), (v) figures given in the *Führer Naval Conferences* documents and by the German naval staff in annexes and appendices, (vi) Churchill (*The Second World War*). They can thus be regarded as reliable.

Table 4

	Tons
Total merchant shipping, 1939	4,500,000
Less 'inland' shipping[1]	1,000,000
Total *seagoing* tonnage (i.e. ocean and coastal)	3,500,000

Of which after one year of war:

Blocked in foreign ports (to May 1940)	1,000,000	
Scuttled or captured (to May 1940).	350,000	
Lost off Norway or subsequently	50,000	
Converted to surface raiders (at sea).	50,000	
Minimum essential for Baltic and Scandinavian trade (incl. iron-ore traffic) and for Norway Occupation Force supply	1,250,000	
Fishing fleet[2]	50,000	
Passenger liners and other vessels unsuitable for Scandinavian traffic and too large for *Sealion*	200,000	
		2,950,000

Balance available in German ports	550,000
Captured in Dutch and Belgian ports .	200,000
Total available for *Sealion* (cargo vessels up to 7,000 tons	750,000

Exact figures for individual categories were subject to considerable fluctuation and adjustment; but the overall picture was clear enough and the *Sealion* cargo-vessel position could thus be summarized:

Tonnage required for first-wave divisions	2,100,000
Total tonnage available	750,000
Deficit	1,350,000

[1] About half the barge fleet required for *Sealion* was obtained from the Low Countries and France. Tugs, barges, lighters and other vessels withdrawn from Germany's inland waterways accounted for more than 800,000 tons.

[2] Reduced to a negligible quantity by September through wholesale withdrawals of trawlers, drifters, etc. to provide naval patrol and escort vessels and additional minesweepers.

[6]

Controversy and Compromise

In the staff discussions between the Army and Navy, if there was much acerbity, there was strictly speaking no controversy – no academic discussion of strategy leading to an inter-service difference of opinion. Räder and the naval staff merely announced the limits of what was possible; and it was the Army leaders who, refusing to accept these limits, kicked furiously against the hard wall of inescapable fact, the fact – never openly mentioned at the conference table – that the scale and scope of *Sealion* had been conditioned, during ten months of maritime warfare, by the Royal Navy's command of the sea.

With something of the petulant obstinacy of a wealthy man rebelling against the sudden necessity to live in reduced circumstances, the Army staff seemed to think that an economy reluctantly conceded in one direction entitled them to continued extravagance in several others. Seven hundred and fifty thousand tons of shipping was only one-third of the tonnage required for their First Wave divisions; but it took them the better part of two weeks to scale the number of divisions down proportionately. And even then they tried to dictate to the naval staff their terms for this concession: '. . . thirteen divisions must attack the English coast on the widest front' – from Ramsgate to Lyme Bay – they 'must be ready for operations in England within . . . two to three days' and, after the first landings, they 'must include sufficient heavy artillery'.

Such terms were regarded by the naval staff not so much as unacceptable for further bargaining as wholly incapable of realization. At the conference of July 21st Räder had been asked to establish: 'To what extent can the Navy safeguard the crossing?' Given the immense disparity in naval strengths, his answer could only be: On a broad front, not at all. In his view the crossing could be protected only if the landings were restricted to a narrow area in the vicinity of Dover or else near

Beachy Head; and at that same conference Hitler had again noted the naval staff's three essential prerequisites: 'complete mastery of the air, the operational use of artillery in the Dover Strait, and protection by minefields'. Only in the Strait could these conditions be satisfied.

On the other hand, given the limited shipping and port facilities available, not even the speediest turn-round could reduce the time required to ferry over the 13 divisions and their initial equipment to less than ten or eleven days. As for heavy artillery, transport difficulties ruled it out since, as Hitler had rightly noted, 'the most difficult part will be the continued reinforcement of material and stores'; and in any event as the naval staff recalled – perhaps with a certain relish – 'the Luftwaffe will do the work of the artillery'.

Grumpily swallowing some of the unpalatable facts forced upon them by the undeniable shortage of transport, the army staff dug their toes in upon the 'broad front'. Ramsgate to Lyme Bay it had to be, nothing less. They would agree to doing without heavy artillery, given the Luftwaffe's assurance that there would be little need for it; they would forego motor transport since it would be difficult to carry over large stocks of petrol and because the Führer had observed that 'we cannot count on supplies of any kind being available to us in England;' they would accept horses as a substitute – 57,000 of them was their requirement. But from the 'broad front' with a landing t dawn they would not budge. When, at an inter-service conference called by Hitler on the last day of the month, Räder reported general progress in technical preparations, he also reported a deadlock in planning, expounded a formidable list of objections to the whole scheme, and boldly threw in a plea for postponement to May 1941.

On this last point, however, Hitler would not give way; the general preparations to meet the invasion date of mid-September must continue. And in fact, apart from the broad-front dispute, things were not going too badly. The Luftwaffe had struck its first blows at ports and shipping along the south coast, causing the enemy considerable losses and depriving him of control over the narrow waters of the Channel. Göring, on Hitler's order, was making ready for the second stage, the gaining of air superiority in south-east England, leading swiftly to the third stage, the massive attacks on airfields and factories, designed to culminate in the devastating assault on London. The Navy, meanwhile, though but few U-boats were available, was scoring notable successes against enemy merchant shipping in the Atlantic owing to the reduced number of British destroyers on escort duty. England was besieged; and a stream of broadcast propaganda was being poured into the ears of her people, alternately cajoling and menacing, explaining the 'hopelessness' of their situation, undermining their defiance. By the time London had felt the full and terrifying weight of Göring's bombs, invasion – against an opposed landing, that is – might have become unnecessary.

Nevertheless, 'an attempt must be made', Hitler decided, 'to prepare the operation for September 15th.' And, what was worse from Räder's viewpoint, 'preparations are to be continued for the attack on a broad basis as originally planned'.

Inter-service planning, tied to this unrealistic decision, remained unsatisfactory. Memoranda passed fruitlessly to and fro, the Army standing firm on all their demands until, on August 7th, at the instigation of the Supreme Command, a meeting was arranged at Army Headquarters at Fontainbleau between the Chiefs of Staff: Halder for the Army, Schniewind for the Navy. The situation was made clear, the naval staff's proposals for a narrow front examined in detail. And at the end, in the luxurious headquarters train on the way back to Paris, Halder exploded with a remark that was later to be unduly stressed.

'I utterly reject the Navy's proposal', he exclaimed. 'From the point of view of the Army, I regard the proposal as complete suicide. I might as well put the landed troops straight through the sausage machine!'

It was not General Halder's exasperated outburst that mattered just then, but Admiral Schniewind's reply. The Navy's plan might seem suicidal, he snapped back, but equally suicidal would be the attempt to transport troops over a wide area – *in view of British naval supremacy.*

There lay the heart of the matter. And in principle there was no way out, for each service was right. The Navy could not effect a safe crossing save on the narrowest of fronts; the Army could not guarantee victory against the re-equipped British land forces save on the broadest. Neither could safely give way; yet the Führer's invasion order still stood, with the provisional warning date only a month ahead. On August 13th Räder took the problem to Hitler.

Save on rare occasions Hitler avoided bringing his three service Commanders-in-Chief to the same conference table. No doubt this was in part due to his determination not to be found in a situation of inferiority, one in which the service chiefs might combine against him and question his decisions. Anything resembling a council of war was not to be tolerated; it would weaken his authority. By separate consultations he was able to keep each in ignorance of the opinions of the other two and to keep them all in uncertainty until, with a crack of the whip – '*I issue the following orders*' – he gathered up the reins and announced the oracular decision, all-knowing, inscrutable, and, so far, infallible.

Thus, at the naval conference held in his Bavarian chalet, the Berghof, on August 13th there were present no more than the usual limited number of personalities. Hitler, as was his custom, sat at the centre of one side of the broad and glossy table; with him were Keitel and Jodl, the naval aide-de-camp, Commander von Puttkamer, in attendance. Across the table Räder and Schniewind faced him and took notes.

Räder opened quietly enough with a straightforward request to the Führer for 'a prompt decision on whether *Operation Sealion* is to be carried out on the wide front proposed by the Commander-in-Chief Army, or on the narrow front proposed by the Commander-in-Chief Navy, as otherwise preparations will be held back'. But once again, although Räder went on to express forcefully his opinion on the demands of the Army, the Führer hesitated. He would not, he said, make a decision until he had conferred with Brauchitsch and Halder on the following day.

None too happy about the state of affairs, Räder played from the same postponement suit from which he had led on July 11th. Summing up the situation he said: 'In view of the limited means available for naval warfare and transport, *Operation Sealion* should, as repeatedly emphasized, be attempted only as a last resort, if Britain cannot be made to sue for peace in any other way.' And he ended by suggesting: 'We must wait and see what effect our intensive air attacks will have.'

Hitler was seldom sincere, even with Räder to whom he spoke openly and almost affably. Concerning his Grand-Admiral's earnest opinion that *Sealion* should be attempted only as a last resort, the conference noted: 'The Führer agrees absolutely.' Yet only two days later, after seeing the Army Commander-in-Chief, he gave orders that preparations for *Sealion* to take place on September 15th were to be continued. He made one important concession: the Army's proposed landing in Lyme Bay was to be abandoned because of 'the inadequate protection available in that area'.

By this time, however, Göring's great 'Eagle-attack' – the *Adlerangriff* – had commenced; within a period of from two weeks to a month the destruction of the enemy air force could be expected, and then would follow the assault on London which, it was hoped, 'would cause the population to flee from the city and block the roads'. With this in mind a paragraph was added to the Führer's decisions of August 15th, ordering both Army and Navy to make their arrangements in such a way 'as not to exclude the possibility of an attack on a narrow front should this be ordered at the last minute'.

Except for Hitler's suggestion, prompted by the Army, that in addition 'it should remain possible to cross once in the direction of Brighton, without further reinforcement' – instead of the naval staff's suggestion of a single landing in the area Dover-Folkestone – this possibility suited Räder's book well enough. A victory for the 'narrow front' plan, its execution would follow those massive air attacks which he had already strongly advocated on July 11th – attacks upon 'harbours and naval bases', upon 'main centres, Liverpool for instance', in conjunction with 'submarine warfare and air attacks on convoys', above all upon the capital with its 'great mass of people who cannot be evacuated'. At the climax, with the people of Britain demoralized, half-starving, her Government tottering, the swift single stroke against the south coast might well tip the scales and start the peace parleys. The dangerous crossing would then become an easy procession, the hard-fought invasion no more than the landing of a token army of occupation.

His hopes were short-lived. Within ten days the Army had reasserted itself, and on August 27th the Führer's decisions were made known. The 'broad front' had won after all. Not, it was true, the initial and impossibly long front; but still long enough – nearly ninety miles – to court disaster should the Royal Navy take a hand in the game.

The landing-areas were defined, laid down in orders. There were four of them: Folkestone to Dungeness – Dungeness to Cliff's End (east of Bexhill) – Bexhill to Beachy Head – Brighton to Selsey Bill. All 13 divisions were to be employed in the First Wave – an impossible number in view of the shipping shortage – with more to follow later to a total of 39. It was to be full-scale invasion with an inadequate transport fleet against a defiant enemy in command of the sea.

With the Luftwaffe already at work over England, with the Army fast completing its preparations and with the target date still set at September 15th, Räder could but comply with the Führer's orders and hasten work on the assembling of the invasion fleet. But he may well have reflected, as he counted his few remaining warships, that the Army was taking an inordinately long time to learn the truth of what Tirpitz had told them twenty-five years earlier, that 'against England the main front is the sea front'.

[7]

Time and the Tides

IN THE EXCHANGE of views between the naval and army staffs
one question at least had been debated seriously and with little
acrimony. Should the crossing be made by day or by night? A
matter of vital importance, there were strong arguments on
either side.

For the Navy the assembly, maintenance in convoy, and
simultaneous bringing to land of many hundreds of vessels
largely unsuited for the navigation of narrow but perilous seas
must at any time be a formidable prospect. That the shepherd-
ing of this huge unpractised fleet could best be accomplished
in daylight appeared self-evident; and by day the expedition,
to a limited extent protected by guns mounted on the French
coast, would be warned by aircraft of the approach of enemy
warships. Admittedly, the Luftwaffe could give no guarantee
that these warships would be destroyed or even stopped, but
should enemy naval vessels draw near to the practically defenceless invasion ships the whole expedition could, in daylight, be
turned back to port without serious loss. Bad for prestige, the
failure could none the less be represented as an experimental
sailing, a menace to be implemented on some more favourable
occasion – or, as Räder might hope, postponed until after the
expected British collapse.

For the Army, however, the prospect of a daylight crossing
contained more than one element of absurdity. It was to be
assumed that isolated enemy reconnaissance aircraft or naval
patrol vessels would give early warning of the fleet's sailing, and
that in any case it would not be long before, in conditions of
normal visibility, the entire assembly could be sighted from the
English coast. Thus, throughout the whole of the daylight hours
the invasion fleet, whether it was attacked or not, would be
under the direct observation of the enemy who could not fail,
during the later stages of the voyage, to note the coastal points

at which it was aimed. All surprise would be eliminated; the enemy would have the best part of the day in which to bring up his troops and organize the counter-attack from land and sea, even supposing his air forces to have been annihilated. Navigational difficulties were the Navy's business; the Army must be bound only by the necessities of land warfare. A night crossing it must be, with an attack at dawn.

Expounded with stubborn military reasoning the case was more or less unanswerable, and the Navy had perforce to agree. The Army did, however, concede that whilst the landings must be made simultaneously before daybreak the moon might be permitted to lighten the darkness. With this in mind the naval staff set about calculating the most suitable dates, around the middle of September, when moon, tide and sunrise should be in favourable conjunction.

The maritime aspect of *Sealion* presented, the naval staff were not slow to discover, a problem of unusual complexity; one that, even discounting enemy interference or the vagaries of the weather, was scarcely capable of positive solution – a sailor's nightmare.

The navigational difficulties – and, whether the Army appreciated them or not, they were immense – were bound to have an important if not decisive influence upon the landings and subsequent military operations. No specially constructed landing craft were available, and of the many hundreds of canal barges to be used for the carrying of the first wave of invasion troops the great majority possessed no means whatever of self-propulsion. More accurately described as lighters, they would have to be towed, in pairs, by some four hundred tugs, unprovided with radar or other wireless aids, towards a coast unlighted and unbuoyed with which their crews were, as a whole, quite unfamiliar. To maintain the coherence of the unwieldy barge groups, to ensure their arrival together at the appointed place and time, the convoy speed must inevitably be low: no more than three knots, it was estimated. At this rate the crossing from Calais or Boulogne to the allotted landing areas between Folkestone and Hastings would occupy a minimum of twelve hours and more probably fifteen; the tides would ebb and flow and start to ebb again between departure and landfall, tides that at their strongest might surpass the speed of the convoys.

But the laying off of a course that should take into account these relative speeds was no simple matter of triangulation. The tidal streams operating in the Dover Strait are not forces of constant strength moving first in one direction and then in the other, unalterable save by the state of the moon. Tide-water flows from the east as well as from the west; the currents are reversed from coast to coast, alter again in mid-Channel, vary from bay to headland. There are eddies and cross-currents; in most areas the local streams are rotary, clockwise, and their strength varies with the strength and direction of the unpredictable wind. In conditions of low visibility corresponding to those of a war-darkened coastline, even the most experienced native navigator might find himself off course and in peril.

Nor, supposing a correct allowance for tidal streams to have been estimated, could a *direct* approach to the landing areas about Dungeness be risked by the barge fleets from Boulogne or Calais. The way is barred by an echelon of banks unmarked in war-time: The Varne, *Les Ridens*, Bullock Bank, The Ridge (*Le Colbart*) – all lying almost in mid-Channel and additional to similar dangers extending from two to three miles off the French coast. Of the principal banks the 'Channel Pilot' has this to say: '*Les Ridens* . . . is indicated by strong ripples when the tidal streams are running with any strength, and by a heavy sea in bad weather.' . . . 'There are strong tide ripples over *The Varne*, and in bad weather a heavy sea, very dangerous to any vessel attempting to cross it.' . . . 'There is much sea on *The Ridge* when the tidal streams are opposed to the wind, and in bad weather there are breakers on the shoalest part. No vessel should attempt to cross it in any circumstances.' Of the accurate following of a circuitous course about these obstacles by the slow and cumbersome barge units, the naval staff had the gravest misgivings.

And that was not all. Although it would be far from the truth to describe the entire coastline marked for invasion as exceptionally dangerous, and although the areas selected for landings were probably the most suitable in Kent and Sussex, it is right to say that as a shore upon which uninitiated mariners were to run their clumsy vessels blindly aground in the darkness of a late September morning it is scarcely hospitable. Of the coast between Selsey Bill and Bognor Regis – to be approached by a fleet of transports and motor-boats from Le Havre – the 'Channel Pilot' says: 'Except near Selsey Bill, no landing can be effected along this part of the coast at low water.' From Bognor eastward to past Littlehampton the direct approach is obstructed by a succession of rocky ledges which either dry at low tide or have over them but two to six feet of water.[1] The harbour at Littlehampton, 'suitable for small vessels accustomed to taking the ground', is obstructed by a sand-bar over which the depth is 'about two feet' and behind which, for some hours on either side of high water, the stream runs at nearly six knots. Farther east, the entrance to Shoreham harbour presents much the same difficulties, with rocks – depths from two to nine feet – instead of sand. In between, Worthing 'has neither harbour nor safe roadstead'. Brighton has nothing to offer other than its two promenade piers, standing in shallow water – and at this time (1940) rendered unusable. Everywhere vessels approaching the coast at night are cautioned to take bearings upon the leading lights – then extinguished – and before entering a harbour 'a vessel without local knowledge is recommended to take a pilot'.

For the invaders the need to secure a port on the west flank at the earliest possible moment would be paramount; but the only one of value – Newhaven – was sure to be well defended and probably blocked; even in time of peace, with its narrow entrance and varying depths, 'no vessel [says the 'Pilot'] should attempt to enter without up-to-date local knowledge', of which the Germans had none. A couple of miles to the east of Newhaven, Seaford road offers good anchorage in stiff sand; and 'good shelter', but only from winds north of east by south and west north-west. Thence, from Seaford to Beachy Head, the

---

[1] The mean draught of the barge-fleet vessels was over six feet fully laden, that of the steam transports up to twenty feet.

foreshore gives little encouragement, since it 'consists mainly of rocky ledges and shingle strewn with boulders fallen from the cliffs above'.

For the landing area from Beachy Head to Bexhill the transports – which, the naval staff estimated, must lie off for some thirty-six hours unloading – providing they had not strayed on to the Royal Sovereign shoals (lying 'from 4 to 8 miles eastward of Beachy Head lighthouse directly in the track of vessels between Beachy Head and Dungeness') would find good holding ground in Eastbourne bay. They would not, however, be able to use the pier, since 'the depth alongside is not more than two feet'; and the bay is sheltered only from offshore winds which are not those prevailing. In front of Bexhill are 'numerous rocky ledges which dry', and much the same is said of St. Leonards-Hastings where several rocky ledges about a quarter of a mile from the shore 'are dangerous to small craft' and where the anchorage off Hastings 'is very open and is not recommended except in fair weather'.

At Rye the harbour has equally little to recommend it to any save local fishermen. The strength and times of tidal streams 'in all parts of the bay must be considered doubtful', but it is known that 'the flood stream runs round the beach at the rate of six knots' and that 'only vessels with local knowledge should attempt the entrance'. Nor is the low-lying shingle promontory of Dungeness easily approachable, least of all on its eastern face where a succession of sandbanks, a mile or two offshore, are covered by no more than two feet to one and a half fathoms of water at low tide. At the eastern extremity of the landing area Sandgate road, off Sandgate some two miles west of Folkestone, 'affords good shelter' but, again, only from offshore winds.

In all this the naval staff could find but cold comfort. The advent of fog, a strong breeze from the south-west, a moderate sea – all likely occurrences at this late season – might disperse the fleet of lighters, cast the motor-vessels away on banks and shoals, and compel the transports to stand out to sea. It was but wise to foresee, without undue pessimism, that the combined hazards of the sea and the coast might well cause a loss of up to 30% in men, material and ships before ever the landing had been achieved and that such loss, and consequent reduction of the capacity to reinforce rapidly, would spell disaster to the expedition as a whole.

Little encouragement was to be gained from the last successful invasion of England. Pevensey bay offers depths of less than five fathoms extending five miles offshore, and 'the anchorage is insecure, owing to the tendency of the wind to back southward in bad weather, when the sea rises rapidly'. How then, the Army may well have asked, had the Duke of Normandy succeeded? For one thing, William had good luck with his weather. For another, his infinitely smaller fleet was composed of shallow-draft vessels every one of which was self-propelled by both oar and sail. His Norman crews had lifelong experience of the Channel coasts whose every creek and inlet they, and their fathers before them, had long explored. Providing the ships kept reasonably well together, the exact time and place of landing mattered little. Above all, both crossing and landing were unopposed.

In an honest attempt to enlighten the Army, Räder had gone into the question of navigational hazards at considerable length during the conference of July 31st, at which Brauchitsch and Halder were present.

'Weather conditions,' he had stressed, 'are of the utmost importance. The naval staff is of the opinion that the transport operation, both as regards the barges to the east and the steamers in the centre and to the west, can be carried out only if the sea is calm. It must be calm enough for the barges to lie almost motionless when landing, as they would immediately spring leaks were they to strike ground or rocks, and this would lead to the destruction of their loads. In the area used for steamer transports, a heavy sea would make it impossible to transfer heavy loads into the barges lying alongside.

'Even if the first wave crosses successfully under favourable weather conditions, there is no guarantee that the same favourable weather will continue through the second and third waves . . . owing to the long intervals between them.'

Neither Hitler nor the Army chiefs appear to have been

moved by this recital of objections which, given the type of vessel to be employed, might well have seemed insuperable to anyone with the least knowledge of the sea. They would not even grant Räder's urgent request for a day-time landing which, although it involved a night-time start, at least permitted an orderly marshalling of the fleet during the crossing.

Of all the various dangers, by night or by day, the naval staff was fully aware. In their memorandum of July 19th they had noted that 'the transport routes lie in a sea area in which weather, fog, current, tides and the state of the sea may present the greatest difficulties', that 'owing to the strong defences of enemy harbours the landing cannot take place there, but the first wave, at least, must land on the open coast', where 'the great navigational difficulties (rise and fall of tide, currents, sea and swell) are obvious', and further, that 'an adequate safety margin as regards mines will not be obtainable in spite of the use of all resources'.

The more the naval staff examined the scheme, the less they liked it and the more they approved their Grand Admiral's desire for postponement. But the Führer had commanded; theirs to obey. Recording their anxieties in the War Diary, they faced the many insoluble problems with considerable courage and heavy hearts.

There was no point in planning for any date *before* the target of September 15th; as Räder had explained, the invasion fleet could be assembled only *by* that date at the earliest. The most suitable S-Day period would therefore be found between the middle and the end of the month. As regards the landing itself, it would be inadvisable to throw barges and lighters ashore at the top of the tide; the next flood might not be sufficient to float them off. So that, allowing for the difference in tidal time between Folkestone and Selsey, two hours after high water would be best; the tidal streams were then relatively weak, some of the rocky offshore dangers would be uncovering, there would be a shorter wait before the next flood and, with it, more water to refloat stranded vessels.

With these considerations in mind it appeared to the staff that the tide served from the 20th to the 26th, with the optimum date the night of the 23rd. Departure would be taken in the evening of S-Day minus 1, the ebb tide adding to the convoy speed and carrying the barge fleets westward down the French coast under the cover of guns and aircraft. After dark the flood would swing them out into mid-Channel; and the moon in its last quarter, rising around 11 p.m., would give some assistance both in sorting out the inevitable confusion and in identifying landmarks as the English shore was neared at about 4 a.m. How the towed lighters would fare during the last hour or two, when their low speed would nearly be matched by that of the falling tide, gave grounds for uneasy conjecture.

[8]

Towards the Climax

ADVISED BY RÄDER of the considered opinion of the naval staff's invasion section, Hitler agreed to the provisional dates. That they should fall later than the one he had stipulated would in fact be of some advantage, for a week's unsettled weather at the end of August had slowed up the Luftwaffe's operations; the first fortnight of September should see Göring's work completed and thereafter the Navy would have the requisite ten days for minesweeping and laying.

The orders, signed by Keitel, were issued from the Führer's Headquarters on September 3rd.

'The following dates for the completion of preparations for *Operation Sealion* have been decided:

1. The earliest day for the sailing of the invasion fleet has been fixed as September 20th, and that of the landing for September 21st.
2. Orders for the launching of the attack will be given on S-Day minus 10, presumably therefore on September 11th.
3. Final commands will be given at the latest on S-Day minus 3 at midday.
4. All preparations must remain liable to cancellation 24 hours before Zero Hour.'

Point 4 was added, no doubt on the insistence of the naval staff, to allow for the sudden onset of inclement weather of whose possibly fatal effect Hitler was now largely aware.

From the day when the *Sealion* plan had grown from a remote possibility to something approaching certainty Räder had missed no opportunity of informing his master on matters concerning the perils of the narrow seas, of wind and weather, of tides and tidal streams. More than a wise precaution, it was a wise topic with which to catch the ear and hold the attention of one so prone to explosive impatience. Mere reiteration at every naval conference of the facts of German naval weakness and shipping shortages, and of their cause, might well have aroused the Führer's wrath and brought – probably behind Räder's back – a damning triple charge of incompetence, cowardice and lukewarm loyalty. With the weather he was on safer ground; even Hitler knew that he had no power over the elements. And the sea remained for him a mystery that, of all his advisers, only Räder could elucidate.

Although well informed on matters pertaining to his Navy, and frequently showing a surprising grasp of technical detail, Hitler was very ignorant of the sea. He had seldom even seen it. His only voyage – a brief one, to Memel, during which he was sick – had been made upon the tideless waters of the Baltic. With Mussolini as host he had glimpsed, at Venice, a glistening arm of the tideless Adriatic. In June, after the fall of France, he had stood for a few minutes silent upon the downy headland near Gris Nez and stared across the Channel at the misty cliffs near Dover, doubtless surmising that they might soon be his. For the rest, his experience of salt water was limited to occasional visits to the naval bases at Kiel and Wilhelmshaven, to rare inspections of units of the fleet, and to a few hours spent upon the deck of his yacht – a luxury thrust upon him more by the need to display his Kaiser-like power than by virtue of the least desire to go to sea.

In the matter of tides and the weather it was, therefore, only natural that he should regard Räder as an invaluable purveyor of facts upon a distasteful topic which he himself was mentally too indolent to study seriously. He was not grateful to his Grand-Admiral – gratitude was not in him – but he was certainly glad of the information supplied; it enabled him to speak with ease and authority to his Generals, to impress them, in phrases culled from Räder, with an apparently surprising depth of knowledge which they did not themselves possess. It was not a very difficult impression to make, for the Generals – and for that matter the entire officer corps – were ignorant of even the simplest of nautical facts.

To the people of Britain – who if they have not, in the romantic phrase, 'got the sea in their blood' have at least got it on their minds – the extent of this ignorance might have given considerable encouragement that summer had they but known the truth. For anyone dwelling in the British islands it is next to impossible to be unaware of the sea. From no point in England is tidal water much more than sixty miles distant; and it is safe to say that all but a very few have at some time visited, travelled upon, paddled in or had some commerce with the sea upon whose safe passage in peace or war their very being depends.

Quite opposite, obviously, is the outlook in Germany. As far as tidal waters are concerned, the North Sea coastal strip is but the narrow neck of a huge sack in which tens of millions of hard-working Germans, living from two to four hundred miles away from salt water, may pass their lives without ever seeing more of the ocean than is shown upon a schoolroom map. Like many an inland people, they can readily be trained to the sea; but not in six weeks.

To professional soldiers in the Nazi Reich what geography had defined history had always seemed to emphasize. Save for the 1914–18 war maritime affairs had hardly ever come into the picture of military operations; nor, in recent years, had a study of them been encouraged by the supreme authority claiming that war against England was highly improbable and that in any case conditions had been changed by the advent of air power. Events had seemed to prove the theory: Poland, the Low Countries, France, had all been conquered by the Army co-operating with the Luftwaffe. Sea power meant nothing any more. Even Norway had been dominated from the air. With the Luftwaffe leading the way against Britain, the invasion crossing would be a brief and probably uneventful episode, the military conquest but a land battle of modest proportions.

When the Army reached the Channel coast and its members saw, the great majority for the first time, how the restless white-capped sea went in and out every few hours, covering and uncovering wide stretches of rock and sand, they stared open-mouthed. The strait was broader than they had expected; save from the short stretch from Boulogne to Calais – and then only on clear days – it was impossible to see the English coast. And when presently, during spells of bad weather, they saw for themselves the steep, choppy seas, the surge of conflicting tidal currents, the driving rain, the obliterating mists, they began to feel a little seasick in advance.

To the Army leaders, however, studying plans on the unemotional map – Rundstedt at Charleville, Brauchitsch at Fontainebleau, Keitel with the Führer in Berlin or at the Berghof – the operation seemed straightforward enough. When the Navy dammed their flooding optimism with 'wholly unacceptable demands' for a narrow front, when Räder lectured on the tides or when, later, the naval staff brought up such details as that, on the morning following S-Day, the lighters would beach some forty minutes later owing to the changing times of those rebellious tides, the Army leaders appeared to regard their objections almost as a personal affront, a sign of inefficiency and weakness on the part of the junior service. Brauchitsch noted it with chagrin in conversation with his Chief of Staff: 'The Navy,' Halder quoted in his diary, 'will not, in all probability, provide us with the means for a successful invasion of England.'

But that was at the end of July, before the narrow-versus-broad front controversy had been settled. Once the compromise had been reached and the landing areas named, even though the front was reduced by a half, the divisions by two-thirds, relations between the services grew happier as the Army came to appreciate, albeit slowly and in limited degree, that the Navy's difficulties concerning transport and the weather might be genuine. Naïve optimism and cocksureness gave way to a more reasoned confidence that was strongly supported in the Supreme Command by the so-called Directorate of National Defence, headed by General Warlimont, where the three services worked harmoniously and strenuously to bring the invasion plan to fruition.

Towards the climax the service chiefs were fortified in their determination to settle accounts with Britain immediately by the fact that Hitler was showing continued interest in making the attack on Russia in the nearest possible future and, should *Sealion* be postponed, even before England had capitulated. At the beginning of August it became known that he had ordered the start of preliminary planning and that, on the 9th, General Warlimont had prepared the first Directive for the eastern campaign; so that, despite an announcement by Jodl on July 29th that the plan had been shelved till May 1941, it began to look as if the Führer might decide to move very much sooner. Fear of a two-front war brought inter-service unanimity on one point; at all costs the war in the west must be finished before another was started in the east.

Preparations for *Sealion* were pushed on apace, training and organization accelerated. By early September it appeared to the Army staff that the tremendous conclusion was not far off; for, dislike and distrust Göring though they did, it seemed certain that the Luftwaffe was on the verge of accomplishing its task. Spells of bad weather and numerous German aircraft losses notwithstanding, the enemy fighters were slowly and surely being beaten down, whilst the pin-prick raids on northern Germany, doing little serious military damage, were arousing the anger of the German people at home and steeling the hearts of front-line troops to the work that lay ahead. Once in England the troops would give short shrift to any who dared to resist, had the enemy's will to fight not already been stamped down by the Luftwaffe acting as artillery.

From scanty intelligence reports it was estimated that there were now some 1,500,000 men in the British armed forces, but that from these only 30 divisions had been organized and trained, of which the majority were short of artillery and tanks. No more than a 'poor' army, Halder deemed it, one that had not yet absorbed the lessons of modern war. Moreover, since it was known that a number of divisions had been allocated to the defence of Scotland, Northern Ireland and Wales, that landings were also feared from Norway and expected in East Anglia, it appeared that little was left to face the attack upon the south coast, which might after all achieve a useful degree of surprise.

For a time the Army staff hopefully included in their plans the employment, air mastery being presumed, of strong forces

of air-landed troops to seize territory inland and hold off the
defenders whilst the beach-heads were being built up. But these
considerable expectations, discouraged by Hitler, were soon
dissipated. For one thing, there were not at that time sufficient
transport aircraft, gliders or parachute troops – there was even
a shortage of parachutes – to provide the substantial forces
required. For another, it became known that the British were
not wholly unprepared for such an eventuality, air reconnaissance having revealed the eclectic assortment of articles – oil
drums, tar barrels, wired poles, posts, cement blocks and the
like – effectively arranged across the English scene wherever
air landings were even remotely possible.

The Army's hopes were finally dashed, however, by Admiral
Schniewind, who pointed out that even an army landed from
the skies would have to be supplied from the sea and that the
matter of seaborne supply was still the weakest point in the
whole *Sealion* plan; nor could airborne troops, he further
explained, help to hold off the British fleet. In the end, only
two small drops were contemplated of about 3,000 men each,
one upon the high ground behind Folkestone to link up with
the Sandgate Bay sea landing, the other (provisional) upon the
downs to the east of Brighton. Even allowing for good weather,
and a lack of vigilance on the part of the defenders, their use-
fulness would be entirely dependent upon the success of the
seaborne invasion which was to precede them.

The Army plans finally laid down by the end of the first week
in September, and modified by the limitations of sea transport,
allowed for from four to six waves of invasion, depending on the
progress of operations in Great Britain (Ireland was included)
during the first month or six weeks, and comprised in all the
total of 40 divisions originally stipulated. Thus spaced, however,
it was estimated that the available sea transport would be fully
sufficient for the task of ferrying, provided that there were no
serious losses in transit. The first wave, in two echelons, consisted of 3 infantry and 1 mountain divisions from the 16th
Army (Busch), based from Boulogne to Rotterdam, and, from
the 9th Army (Strauss), of 2 infantry and 1 mountain divisions

from the neighbourhood of Abbeville and 2 infantry divisions from Rouen. Of these 9 divisions the first (assault) echelon included only elements totalling some 60,000 men, to be distributed to the four landing areas along the Sandgate to Brighton coast in the proportion of 2, 2, 2, 3; the area west of Brighton to Selsey Bill being excluded from the first assault and left either to the second echelon or to the second wave depending on the success of the first landings. Two infantry divisions from the 6th Army (Reichenau), based on Rennes and St. Lô, would be held in readiness to move subsequently from Cherbourg to Lyme Bay.

Among the arms and equipment to be landed with the first echelon at dawn on S-Day were some 250 light amphibious tanks. There seems to be no doubt that these machines could either float in calm water or, for a limited number of a special hermetically sealed type, crawl short distances over the smooth bottom of a shallow sea; but there had been little time for testing and training, and how they would have fared in the rough water and moderately heavy surf to be expected on the English Channel coast in autumn is at least problematical. It does not appear probable that very many of such novel and untried vehicles would have survived in a breaking sea the hazards of shoals, rocky ledges and shingle banks.

Some forty barges had been decked over and adapted to accommodate the 17 anti-aircraft batteries which the Army deemed essential to the assault in view of the almost complete lack of artillery. For the crossing the guns were provided, on their improvised ferries, with dual-purpose mountings enabling them to fire at either aircraft or surface vessels; but here again time had been too short for serious training or practice, so that accurate laying from the unaccustomed platform of a river barge wallowing in mid-Channel seemed rather more than improbable.

Other weapons of value to the first echelon invaders, supposing that they could bring them to land, included a score or more of 6-barrel rocket-projectors (whose maximum range was said to be 6,000 metres) and something over 50 light mountain guns. Once a lodgment had been secured several thousand bicycles and the first batch of some 2,000 horses would give the landed forces a measure of mobility; but the unloading of this equipment and these animals, together with the tanks and anti-aircraft guns, was bound to be costly in time and effort, so that apart from all considerations of weather and of enemy intervention at sea it seemed likely that for the first few hours after a landing the attack would have to rely mainly upon the rifles, machine guns and mortars of a few thousand infantry.

The bringing across of this first echelon would occupy, in round numbers, 45 steam transports, 650 barges and lighters, 215 tugs and 550 motor vessels, a total of nearly 1,500 vessels excluding the minesweeper and torpedo-boat escort. Approaching the English coast on a front of 70 miles, and necessarily deploying in line as they neared the beaches, there would thus be one vessel to every 80 yards – a mean density which could scarcely pass unobserved by the defenders either on land or at sea. So evenly spaced an alignment of the entire invasion fleet might be highly improbable – there would be wide gaps in some areas and confused bunching in others – but for observation by the defence there would be plenty of time, given the last two hours of the crossing when the average speed of the barge convoy against the ebb could hardly exceed two knots.

The second echelon, with the greater part (roughly two-thirds) of the 9 divisions in the first wave, together with all their vehicles, would require the maximum number of vessels available in the invasion fleet and these would absorb the entire port facilities from Ostend to Le Havre. Subsequently, if the operation were to be successful, an uninterrupted shuttle service would have to be maintained day and night by all vessels for at least a week. It was a lot to expect. Well might Räder stress that there was 'no guarantee' of so long a period of favourable weather when, by favourable, he meant flat calm.

From all this it is not to be supposed that those in the front line of *Sealion*, the staff and executive ranks and the men of the 9 divisions, were in any way despondent at the prospect of invasion. The crossing might be perilous; so had it been for Julius Caesar. Morale was still high, training and equipment appeared adequate for the task, unquestioning discipline was reinforced by complete confidence in the High Command. Let them but get moving, land the first two echelons, get their weapons and supplies ashore – and, once in England, they would build up strength, fend off the British hamstrung by the Luftwaffe, and break out to reach the Portsmouth-Gravesend line beyond which lay total victory and *Heil Hitler!*

Once in England. . . . Between the dream and the reality a great gulf was fixed. The Army leaders for the most part ignored it; Hitler failed to comprehend it and pinned his faith to the claims of air power. Only Räder and his Admirals had measured its depth.

[9]

The Burden of Admiralty

I

IN ENGLAND THAT summer there were few who did not recall
the recurrent challenge across the centuries, the invasion threats
of Spain and the Armada, of France, of the Dutch, of Napoleon.
The enemy, too, remembered. Long afterwards Rundstedt
admitted that in those momentous days he often thought of how
Napoleon had been baffled. He failed to add, however, that
what he – and military experts the world over – believed at the
time was that the sea power that had baffled Napoleon had
been superseded by German air power.

It was not a belief to which the naval staff could subscribe,
even when they agreed with Räder that the destruction of vital
ports such as London and Liverpool might hasten Britain's
downfall. For them, in the matter of *Sealion*, 'the main front was
the sea front'; and since, when they thought of Napoleon, they
also remembered Nelson, in the comparison between the events
of 1805 and those of 1939–40 they may have found an unhappy
contrast.

In the summer of 1805 Napoleon, having assembled his army
at Boulogne, set in motion the series of manoeuvres – by his
fleets at Brest, Rochefort, in the Spanish ports and at Toulon –
designed to confuse and draw off the blockading forces of Corn-
wallis in the Atlantic and Nelson in the Mediterranean and to
culminate in a concentration of French ships in the Channel
so as to obtain that mastery of the narrow seas essential for
invasion. When, at the close of the Trafalgar campaign – before
ever the battle that sealed it was fought – the Emperor saw that
the manoeuvres had failed of their purpose he wisely abandoned
the plan to invade, withdrew his troops from Boulogne, and
turned east.

In 1940, Hitler, having first subdued western Europe, turned
to the invasion of England at a time when the cumulative effects

of the ten months' campaign at sea had deprived him – temporarily, but at the crucial moment – of almost all naval power and of nearly half his sea-going merchant shipping. On the analogy with Napoleon, he took up the planning of invasion *after* Trafalgar. Regarded as a question of sea power – and this was to be a seaborne invasion – the affair planned for September was hopeless from the start.

By the supporters of *Sealion*, however, it was argued that the lack of German sea power could be made good by air power, that the Luftwaffe was strong enough to hold off the enemy ships during the relatively brief period of the crossing, and thereafter, as indicated in Hitler's directive, 'to do the work of artillery' ahead of the advancing troops. Whatever conditions prevailed upon the high seas, here in the Channel, they claimed, air power was dominant; it *was* sea power. To disprove this view, to define the limits of air power, of what the Luftwaffe could and could not do, was the slow and painful task thrust upon the naval staff even as they worked day and night to create and assemble that invasion fleet in the likelihood of whose success they could not believe.

They did not have to convince Göring who, from the moment when Hitler – in Directive 17[1] – ordered the intensified air attack, set out to conquer England by himself, without the least regard for the progress of *Sealion*. But to convince the High Command of the Army needed more than Räder's sensible arguments and lucid explanations. Ignorant of the elementary facts concerning sea power they remained unenlightened almost to the end.

The main purposes of British naval strategy in a major war are worth recalling at this point. They are:

1. First and foremost, to keep open the vital trade routes so that, maintaining the sea-power chain (Production-Shipping-Markets), the inhabitants of the British Isles shall not starve.
2. To deny sea routes, commercial or military, to the enemy.

[1] Discussed in subsequent chapters and given in full at Appendix A.

3. To transport or convoy armed forces and supplies to any Government-selected theatre of operations.
4. To prevent or defeat, in conjunction with the other services, an invasion of Great Britain.

An enemy's opposition to or interference with any of these purposes will create opportunities for bringing him to action, but against a determined and powerful foe possessing surface, air and submarine weapons, and the industrial resources to maintain them, it is not to be expected that any single engagement will dispose of the opposition to all four purposes at one and the same time. The 'battle' is continuous, from the war's beginning to the war's end, since it is improbable that all the purposes will have been fully accomplished or secured before overall victory in the war has been won.

It must further be noted that even in peace-time the naval force necessary to exercise the immense and penetrating influence of British sea power has a more active role to play than either of the other armed services. It must at all times be ready and immediately available to ensure that steady flow of shipping without which the island people would perish almost overnight.

In September 1939 it was apparent to the Admiralty that the burden about to be imposed upon the Royal Navy would be a weighty one. With world-wide responsibilities and several potential enemies, Britain had but one ally; and although the British fleet was still the most powerful in the world its deficiencies were manifold and disquieting. These deficiencies were largely due to the parsimony forced upon successive Governments by the fond belief of the British people and Parliament that after the ruinous experiences of the First World War no great powers would ever want to fight each other again and that, if they did, the League of Nations would soon stop them. Thus, when war came – and for at least four years it had been plain to clear-sighted observers that it would come – the ships, however ready the crews, were too old and too few. Of 15 capital ships all but 2 were of first-war construction or design, and if some had been modernized all were inferior in speed to the newer enemy ships of approximately equivalent class. The minimum number of cruisers essential to the protection of British world trade had been put officially at 70; there were 58, many of them far from new. The number of destroyers and escort vessels in service towards the end of the First World War had been well over 400; there were now barely 200, some of them elderly. Only 1 modern aircraft-carrier was in commission, the other 4 were first-war conversions; and the new carriers, as well as the 5 new replacement battleships, were not expected to be ready for service for another year to eighteen months.

Against this the enemy – however much Räder might deplore Hitler's premature opening of hostilities that had put an end to Germany's massive building programme – could oppose a force which, as yet numerically weak, contained many elements of strength. True, the curtailment of the programme as well as the shortage of naval dockyards had prevented the building of a balanced fleet; there was, for instance, a notable deficiency of destroyers. But this very weakness, ruling out the possibility of challenging the Royal Navy to a fleet engagement, had suggested to Räder, the expert in cruiser warfare, the use of his more powerful units as commerce raiders. For this purpose there were, shortly after the outbreak of war, the 3 pocket-battleships, 2 battleships (*Scharnhorst, Gneisenau*) and 2 heavy cruisers, any one of which let loose upon the trade routes could – whilst unable, as Räder knew, to achieve a decisive result – work serious mischief in the early stages of the war.

But, dislocation of trade apart, it was the drawing off of British naval power from the accomplishment of its other main purposes that constituted the principal value of the surface raider. Comparing the qualities of the heavy ships in each navy it was evidently not far from the truth to claim, as did the German naval staff, that any British ship powerful enough to destroy, say, a pocket battleship would not be fast enough to catch her. A single surface raider at large upon the vast spaces of the Atlantic Ocean would therefore impose an altogether disproportionate strain upon the already insufficient British cruiser forces.[1]

---

[1] In October, 1939, to hunt the *Deutschland* (later renamed *Lützow*) and *Graf Spee*, there were detached from the Allied fleets 4 British and French battleships, 5 aircraft carriers and 14 cruisers.

And then there were the U-boats, built by virtue of the Anglo-German Naval Agreement of 1935, that ill-advised act of appeasement whereby Britain combined with Nazi Germany to flout the Versailles Treaty and thus – despite official assurances by the British Government that the submarine weapon had been 'mastered' – permitted the re-creation of the threat eliminated in 1918. The Germany Navy started the war with but 57 U-boats in commission, but she started it with the determination to use them offensively against trade and – save, briefly, as a matter of political propaganda – no nonsense about international agreements. Soon a steady toll was being taken, once again, of British and neutral shipping; only the early vacillations in the U-boat building programme delayed the development of what was, for Britain, the deadliest peril of all.

These dangers to world-wide responsibilities already in the first half-year severely testing the resources of the Royal Navy were as nothing to the situation that arose in two brief months from the conquest of Norway to the fall of France. Suddenly the coasts of Scandinavia and of the Low Countries and France took on the appearance of monstrous jaws, toothed with U-boats and cruisers and the bomber groups of the Luftwaffe, ready to close upon Britain and crunch out life. Or so it seemed to contemporary historians. For it is the measure of the Royal Navy's wholly admirable achievement that – stretched to the limit of elasticity, faced with the now open hostility of Italy, the growing enmity of Japan and the doubtful neutrality of Spain – it had, at the very time when Hitler was creating *Sealion*, largely fulfilled the four main purposes of naval strategy.

Between September 1939 and end of July 1940 the Royal Navy had:

1. Kept open the trade routes, despite surface raiders and U-boats upon which it had inflicted severe losses.
2. Escorted large numbers of troops to France and to other war theatres, and brought back to Britain over 500,000 British and Allied troops and a not inconsiderable quantity of material from France, including 300 guns and over 2,000 vehicles.

3. Denied the use of ocean routes to the enemy, depriving him of nearly half of his sea-going merchant tonnage.

4. Accounted, temporarily at least, for the greater part of the German fleet.

But these things were far from constituting the sum total of the Royal Navy's achievements. Not only had the great majority of the troops evacuated from Dunkirk, from the Channel ports and the Atlantic harbours travelled upon the decks of its warships, but its escort vessels great and small had also brought to the homeland fresh divisions from Canada, Australia and New Zealand. Over and above the normal requirements of trade and food supply it had convoyed to Britain cargoes of urgently needed war material, of aircraft from America, of the all-essential oil and petrol without which the Royal Air Force could not fly. It had brought in during July a hoard of surplus arms from the United States – including 500,000 rifles, 80,000 machine and sub-machine guns, and 900 guns – wherewith to re-equip the mostly disarmed divisions from Dunkirk and western France. Hastening the repair of damaged ships and the completion of new ones, and absorbing the air-war lessons learnt off Norway and Dunkirk, it had redeployed its forces to meet the new menace.

By September it could thus be said that the Royal Navy – together, of course, with the Merchant Navy – had by its own exertions rendered an immediate, large-scale and nourished invasion from the sea virtually impossible. It had reduced the German merchant tonnage to a quantity insufficient to carry over an army strong enough to be certain of defeating the considerable British army which sea power had helped to re-equip. It had reduced the German naval forces to a point where they could safeguard neither an initial crossing nor a subsequent reinforcement. Only two contingencies could render nugatory the Navy's role in preventing or defeating *Sealion*: a sustained and destructive air attack with maximum strength upon all naval bases and dockyards as well as upon individual ships in home waters, or national surrender through a sudden collapse of morale. The first was, for reasons to be discussed later, a practical impossibility; and in any case Göring had no intention of undertaking it, nor had he any explicit orders to do so. The second, given the temper of the nation and the quality of its leadership, did not seem very probable.

Seaborne raids upon weakly defended stretches of the coast the Navy made no claim to be able to prevent; it had never pretended that it could, even in less critical periods of history; and the Admiralty, unaware of the extent of the enemy's maritime weakness, thought it only wise to warn the other services that such raids might be numerous and individually important. In July the First Sea Lord (Admiral Sir Dudley Pound) told the Prime Minister that 'it appears probable that a total of some hundred thousand men might reach these shores without being intercepted by naval forces'; but he went on to admit that their supply – 'unless the German Air Force had overcome both our Air Force and our Navy' – seemed practically impossible. Churchill, rightly anxious to make assurance doubly sure, then suggested that the Chiefs of Staff and Home Defence should consider a force of 200,000 invaders distributed, as the First Sea Lord had imagined, over five coastal areas from the north of Scotland to the south-west of England. But wise though such precautionary studies might be in order to put the Chiefs of Staff and of Home Defence on their mettle, they in no way corresponded to the realities of the enemy's situation: he had neither sufficient transports for such large-scale raids nor the warships to protect them. Of this, however, no one in Britain could then be sure.

II

One other danger threatening the Royal Navy might still favour *Sealion* decisively. The shortage of ships, especially of destroyers, was acute; in the immediate future everything might depend upon their correct disposition.

In all naval areas the demands were clamant. From the Norway coast to the Biscay ports surface raiders and U-boats though few in number could now menace the Atlantic lifeline. With Italy in the war, and France out of it, the short road to Egypt and the Canal was all but blocked; Gibraltar and Malta were imperilled. In the far east Japan was growing restless. And at the centre of the British world there loomed up from across the North Sea and over the Channel, from points a thousand and more miles apart, the near-certainty of an attempt at invasion.

Upon the Admiralty staff the weight of responsibility lay heavily. Of possibly vital importance might be their estimates of the strength and intentions of the German fleet – of the state of whose major warships they were far from certain, even in August – and of the scale, direction and timing of the expected attack. Accurate information was hard to come by; submarine patrols now yielded little save loss; long-range air reconnaissance, frequently hindered by cloudy weather, was intermittent and none too reliable; secret agents on the Continent had mostly been eliminated or had gone to ground, new organizations had yet to be created. Would the invasion aim at East Anglia and the Kentish promontory as General Brooke supposed; at Scotland, the Shetlands, even Iceland, as Admiral Pound suggested; or – as Churchill thought whilst naming the Wash to Dover as the most dangerous area – at all these and Ireland as well? Faulty assessment of scant intelligence; too wide a dispersal of available force or too distant a concentration; excessive caution under the threat, perhaps exaggerated, of enemy air power, coupled with too sympathetic a hearing of the claims of Atlantic convoy – these likely errors might, that autumn, spell the doom of Britain.

Paradoxically, it was an erroneous appreciation that assured Britain's safety, the false alarm that gave the alarm. By naval and military authorities it was regarded as certain that Germany had been preparing for invasion since long before the war and as even more certain, once Hitler had reached the coast on May 20th, that invasion was about to be attempted. This deep conviction had, initially, nothing to give it support other than the same imagination which had conjured up a similar peril in the First World War and which dated back to the unfounded 'scares' of the early years of the century. Churchill was later to write that he had 'an inkling in June' of the German plans,[1] but

[1] *The Second World War*, Vol. II, page 267.

since no plans were even outlined by the Supreme Command until after July 2nd it would seem that for 'inkling' one may read 'intuition'. Certain it is that until the first week in September knowledge of the *Sealion* intention was little else than guesswork; for if there were rumours a-plenty, many of them disseminated by the enemy, early visual observation of an invasion fleet that had not yet been assembled was scarcely possible. When Churchill praised 'our excellent intelligence'[1] for supplying advance information of the enemy's plans he was being magnanimous; less modestly he might have claimed the use of his own 'intelligent anticipation'.

But if the guesses were often wrong in detail, the profound belief in the enemy's preparedness stimulated the taking of urgent defence measures and ensured that invasion, when it came, would come as no surprise.

. The Admiralty, confronted with an ancient threat enhanced by the menace of air attack, reacted in the traditional manner. The historic precedents of former wars had long established the principles. Nelson had formulated them in 1801; they were restated by Churchill in a Minute written on August 5th, 1940.[2]

1. Our first line of defence against invasion must be as ever the enemy's ports. Air reconnaissance, submarine watching, and other means of obtaining information should be followed by resolute attacks with all our forces available and suitable upon any concentrations of enemy shipping.

2. Our second line of defence is the vigilant patrolling of the sea to intercept any invading expedition, and to destroy it in transit.

3. Our third line is the counter-attack upon the enemy when he makes any landfall, and particularly while he is engaged in the act of landing. This attack, which has long been ready from the sea, must be reinforced by air action; and both sea and air attacks must be continued so that it becomes impossible for the invader to nourish his lodgments. . . .

[1] *ibid.*, page 261.
[2] Quoted in *The Second World War*, Vol. II, pages 257 *et seq.*

The validity of these principles, already set forth in detailed Admiralty instructions at the end of May, was unchallengeable; their application was far from easy. At the time when the Minute was written nothing certain was known of the enemy's plans, and attempts to invade from any, or all simultaneously, of the areas outlined by the First Sea Lord were still envisaged: from the Bay of Biscay, from the Channel, from Dutch and Belgian ports, from German ports, from Norway. For the application of paragraphs 1 and 2, the vessels principally required for the 'vigilant patrolling' of five considerable sea areas were destroyers; and ten times the number available would not have been too many. Audacity and aggressive action were in the traditions of the Navy and helped to maintain morale, but they were bound to be costly at a time when any loss could ill be afforded. [At the end of August, for instance, of a flotilla of destroyers endeavouring to intercept an enemy minelaying force forty miles north-west of the Texel, two (*Esk*, *Ivanhoe*) were sunk and a third (*Express*) seriously damaged by mines, and little harm done to the foe.] Until more was known of enemy intentions slender naval resources could not constantly be hazarded in proximity to enemy-held shores; yet unless they were hazarded the intentions, movements and shipping concentrations could scarcely be discovered. It was something of a dilemma, made no less acute by the sharp division of opinion regarding the disposition of warships between the Admiralty and the Commander-in-Chief Home Fleet, Admiral Sir Charles Forbes.

Since the beginning of May the draining away of strength from the Home Fleet into other Commands had been almost continuous. The conquest of the Low Countries and the Channel ports had drawn southward an increasing number of the smaller ships; at Dunkirk destroyers, principally, and other light naval vessels had lifted more than half of the 338,000 men evacuated and had suffered the heaviest losses. With the entry of Italy into the war and the neutralization of the French fleet, the reinforcement of the Mediterranean had become urgently necessary; battleships, cruisers, the *Ark Royal* were despatched to strengthen the eastern area centred upon Alexandria and to create the new Force H at Gibraltar. In home waters, with the

five-point invasion threat in mind, the Admiralty detached
further cruisers to southern areas and moved still more destroyers to the zone of greatest danger: the Wash-Dover line. By
the end of July the cruiser and destroyer strength of the Home
Fleet had been so reduced as seriously to restrict its normal
functions.

These functions were the same as hitherto, but their burden
had grown infinitely heavier. Cover had still to be provided for
Atlantic convoys entering the narrowed lane of the North-
Western Approaches. The immensely lengthened patrol line to
the north of the British Isles had to be guarded, the Norwegian
coast kept under observation, the sea routes as far as possible
denied to the enemy, the expected surface raiders intercepted.
Protection had to be extended to areas as far apart as Northern
Ireland, the Faeröes, Iceland, any of which might be the object
of enemy attack and all of which were vital to control of the
Atlantic routes. And at the same time a balanced fleet of battleships, cruisers, destroyers and aircraft had to be maintained
ready for action against a possibly strong force of enemy warships moving across the North Sea in conjunction with the
expected east coast invasion. Small wonder that Admiral Forbes,
anxiously watching his dwindling command, expressed his
alarm to the Admiralty and inquired, a touch ironically, just
how many ships it was intended to leave him.

The Admiralty, however, had little choice. Invasion appeared
to threaten most immediately in the south-east. Early warning
of departure from the Low Countries or from German ports
could not be depended upon; in unpredictable weather conditions air reconnaissance had proved unreliable; 'vigilant
patrolling' to intercept on passage or to counter-attack after a
landing must be undertaken by small craft backed by destroyers,
themselves supported by cruisers. Until new or repaired ships
came from the dockyards, these cruisers and destroyers could
be obtained only from one source. The withdrawals from the
Home Fleet were maintained.

And yet the seriously weakened Home Fleet was still expected
to provide in the north a battle force sufficient to counter any
forward move by German naval forces whose strength continued

to be largely a matter of guesswork. The action to be taken by the Fleet was defined by the Admiralty on July 20th, the first point being in the nature of a concession:

> 'Their Lordships do not expect our heavy ships to go south to break up an expedition landing on our coast in the absence of any reports indicating the presence of enemy heavy ships.'

The second point, however, was an order to action:

> 'If enemy heavy ships support an expedition, accepting the risks involved in an approach to our coast in the southern part of the North Sea, then it is essential that our heavy ships should move south against them, also accepting risks.'

This talk of enemy 'heavy ships' gives the measure of the lack of accurate information concerning the German Navy, which was to endure throughout the invasion crisis. The Prime Minister, whilst taking a serious view of the invasion threat in his Notes and Minutes, tended to write off the enemy heavy ships and indeed almost the whole of the German Navy; but, although his view was not far removed from the truth (see above, 'The Light Cruiser Squadron'), it was at variance with the intelligence reaching the naval staff. Belated photographic reconnaissance eventually showed the twin battleships *Scharnhorst* and *Gneisenau* in dry dock at Kiel, together with the *Lützow*, but the extent of their respective injuries was unknown; and in the same port was the new heavy cruiser *Prinz Eugen*, said to be commissioning and ready for sea. At Hamburg lay the uncompleted *Bismarck*; believing her to be far more advanced than in fact she was, the Admiralty feared she might be operational by September. At Wilhelmshaven the *Tirpitz* was a long way from completion and could be considered 'safe'; but the *Scheer*, refitting, appeared to be ready. The *Hipper's* shortcomings and injuries were unknown; the light cruisers had returned from Norway; destroyers were few, but there might be as many as ten or twelve, and a score of U-boats. Even the two antique battleships – *Schlesien, Schleswig-Holstein* – were in commission and might be brought forward under air cover and escorted by torpedo craft and minelayers.

Thus at the worst – and the worst had to be faced – a very powerful squadron might be available to the enemy in the immediate and most dangerous future, before the Army was ready to repel an invader, before new British ships had come forward, older ones been repaired or refitted; a squadron headed by the mighty *Bismarck* and including a pocket battleship and two heavy cruisers. One or more of these heavy ships creeping up the Norwegian coast to break out into the Atlantic might draw off Home Fleet ships at a critical moment and, if not caught, work fatal mischief upon the unguarded convoys. Alternatively, or perhaps concurrently, the squadron, or part of it, might support the invasion in the southern North Sea where its intervention, however costly to itself, might be decisive unless promptly dealt with. To guard against the danger of a break-out to the north Scapa was still the best station, but against the alternative the Admiralty provided, in agreement with Admiral Forbes, that in the event of a report of imminent invasion the Fleet should move from Scapa to Rosyth; the Forth being designated as the southern limit of heavy ships' station and the approximate line Wash-Texel as the southern limit of heavy ships' action.

These were wise precautions, and the fact that they were taken because of a serious over-estimate of what was in reality no more than a ghost squadron, though it exercised the minds of the naval staff, made little difference to the Admiralty's overall arrangements. With the near-certainty of an invasion attempt before autumn as the main preoccupation, and with resources stretched to the limit, the general disposition of available ships in home waters could scarcely have been bettered.

About the 2,000-mile perimeter of Britain there were ranged, from the end of July on, upwards of a thousand armed patrol vessels – sloops, gunboats, motor torpedo-boats, minelayers, anti-submarine trawlers, drifters – of which, Churchill noted, 'two or three hundred are always at sea', with a good proportion on the most threatened east and south-eastern seaboard where the bulk of the cruisers and destroyers was also stationed. A Town-class cruiser (twelve 6-inch) patrolled from the Forth to the Humber, a second from the Humber to the Thames; at

Sheerness were two light cruisers of the *Aurora* class (six 6-inch). Here, at Sheerness and Harwich, in the Nore Command under Admiral Drax[1] was concentrated the main destroyer force: some 30 vessels and a number of corvettes.

Neither cruisers nor destroyers were maintained at Dover after July owing to the dangers of air attack and of bombardment from the neighbourhood of Cape Gris Nez; but at Portsmouth were stationed a Town-class cruiser and upwards of a dozen destroyers. The withdrawal of destroyers did little to diminish the activity of Dover under the command of Admiral Sir Bertram Ramsay. Up to forty armed vessels were constantly available, including MTBs and gunboats, minesweepers, anti-submarine trawlers and other auxiliaries. In close co-operation with the Nore, these small ships maintained a tireless watch in the Dover Strait during the dark hours whilst, from the cliffs, enemy shipping movements between Calais and Boulogne were kept under daily observation.

In August the battleship *Revenge* (eight 15-inch, twelve 6-inch) arrived at Plymouth to join another Town-class cruiser and a division of destroyers. In the Western Approaches Command, still based at Plymouth, the remaining destroyers on convoy duties in the Atlantic escorted only as far as 300 miles west of Ireland, so that the majority being at any given moment well within this limit they could swiftly be recalled, either to the mouth of the Channel or – with the southern entrance to the Irish Sea closed by British minefields – to Northern Ireland, over which a County-class cruiser (eight 8-inch) stood guard with numerous small craft in the Firth of Clyde.

At Scapa lay the Home Fleet, its strength frequently varying, but including for the critical period the battleships *Nelson*, *Rodney* (nine 16-inch each), the battle-cruisers *Hood* (eight 15-inch) and *Repulse* (six 15-inch), the carrier *Furious* (thirty-three aircraft), 2 County-class, 1 Town-class and 2 light cruisers, and 2 destroyer flotillas. Limited air power was also available from the Navy's land-based Fleet Air Arm and from the Coastal Command of the Royal Air Force. Despite an inadequate destroyer screen, it was, given the restrictions imposed by

[1] Admiral the Hon. Sir Reginald Plunkett-Ernle-Erle-Drax.

pressing needs elsewhere, a temporarily sufficient battle force.[1]

All things considered, it can therefore be asserted that the Royal Navy at this time was ready and able to defeat any practicable invasion attempt from the sea. Its ships were well distributed to meet all probable and some improbable threats, well dispersed to lessen the expected damage from air attack – of which, however, there were few signs, save briefly and sporadically on the south coast in July and at the beginning of August. Its lines of concentration were short enough to allow any threatened area to be covered by light forces, at worst within ten hours', at best within two or three hours' steaming. The cruisers could all make 32 knots, the destroyers 32 to 37; even if they failed, through too brief a warning, to intercept on passage, the 8- and 6-inch guns of the cruisers, the 4·7-inch and torpedo tubes of the destroyers would make short work of either stranded invasion craft or moored transports, as well as of intended reinforcements to any landing point once known.

Strong enough to meet the *imagined* enemy force, the Navy's concentrations were in fact almost too strong for the *real*. Insufficient consideration was given to the limiting factor of German merchant tonnage, too much to the supposed power of a temporarily non-existent German fleet. And although the naval staff, fearful of complacency, were wise to warn the Army that the Navy could not guarantee the inviolability of the British shores, some were inclined to overstate the newly appreciated dangers of air power in a manner which made General Brooke think that command of the sea was a thing of the past. And yet at Dunkirk out of some 40 destroyers, making many voyages to rescue 100,000 men, only 4 had been sunk and about 20 damaged in the course of ten days' heavy attack by dive-bombers; and even so the losses had mostly been inflicted upon ships stopped or moving slowly close inshore over a narrow, well defined area. Moving at full speed across a sea 'front' 100 miles long by 20 miles wide at its narrowest, and more than

---

[1] None of the above stationings should be taken as hard and fast; changes were many and frequent. The disposition of ships on September 14th is shown on the map at the end of the volume.

Grand-Admiral Räder, C.-in-C., German Navy
European Picture Service, New York

Admiral Schniewind, Chief of German Naval Staff
Associated Press

SEALION OBJECTIVES

WEST FLANK

A. Brighton – Newhaven

B. Newhaven – Beachy Head

C. Beachy Head – St Leonards

EAST FLANK

D. Hastings – Dungeness (on skyline upper right)

E. Dungeness – Hythe

Photos: Aerofilms Ltd

THE GERMAN SURFACE FLEET

SEPTEMBER 1940

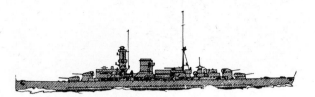

ADMIRAL HIPPER
heavy cruiser

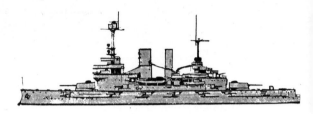

SCHLESIEN
SCHLESWIG-HOLSTEIN
old battleships

NÜRNBERG
light cruiser

KÖLN
light cruiser

EMDEN
light cruiser (training)

Eight destroyers ready for sea

Jane's Fighting Ships

BARGE ASSEMBLIES, September 1940. Boulogne (*left*), Dunkirk (*right*). Some 200 barges can be identified in these two ports, in addition to more than a score of small craft at Boulogne.

By courtesy of Imperial War Museum

THE BRITISH ADMIRALS

DRAX – *The Nore*

B. RAMSAY – *Dover*

JAMES – *Portsmouth*

POUND – *First Sea Lord*

FORBES – *Home Fleet*

Photos by courtesy of Imperial War Museum except DRAX (*Debenham & Gould*)

BRITISH WARSHIPS I

REVENGE – *battleship*

SOUTHAMPTON – *town-class cruiser*

AURORA – *light cruiser*

Jane's Fighting Ships

ACHERON – *Acasta class* (destroyer). *Jane's Fighting Ships*

Left: AFRIDI – *Tribal class* (destroyer). *Wright & Logan Southsea*
Right: JERSEY – *Javelin class* (destroyer). *Wright & Logan, Southsea*

Left: EREBUS – (monitor). *John I. Thorneycroft, Southampton*
Right: Vosper-built M.T.B. *Vosper Ltd, Portsmouth*

100 miles wide on either flank, operating chiefly at night against an almost undefended mass of transports, losses could hardly be heavier than during the evacuation and would certainly, in so vital a matter as invasion, be endurable. That the German naval staff were persuaded of this, believing – as their own records show – that aircraft would have little success in defending the invasion fleet, was something which the British Chiefs of Staff might have been surprised to learn.

Had it been possible to evaluate correctly these facts of enemy weakness, it might well have been found advisable to release to Admiral Forbes some of those destroyers and anti-submarine trawlers for which he so urgently, and justifiably, appealed for work in the north-western approaches where diminished escorts had led to a greatly increased total of merchant-ship sinkings. But the faults – and responsibility for them must rest upon Churchill as Prime Minister and Minister of Defence, as well as upon the First Sea Lord, Admiral Pound – were, in the matter of *Sealion*, on the right side. So much was unknown; the German armed forces had shown in the recent past an unerring capacity for seizing the initiative and for snatching victory before their enemies had time to recover from the shock. Given the conviction that they had planned invasion before the war, it seemed hard to credit that they had not devised some new and cunning method, some 'secret weapon' – a heavier bomb, a deadlier mine, an unsinkable landing craft. From the need to guard against a fatal surprise by sea not a man could be spared, not a ship released. The Cromwellian imperative, 'Neglect no means', ruled the day.

Thus, when in the first week of September the German transports began slipping down the Belgian coast into the Channel ports and the emphasis was shifted from the south-east to the southern seaboard, little change was found necessary in the general arrangements; hardly a ship had to be moved. The dispositions were about to stand a momentous test; events would prove whether or not they were the right ones.

For a while opinion at the Admiralty was divided on the question of the probable timing of the assault. When, early in August, Admiral Forbes proposed a raid on Bear Island with ships of the Home Fleet, the Admiralty advised postponement because 'for another week it will be a moonless period which we have always considered most likely for an invasion'. A month later, however, watching the weather, the tides and the state of the moon with the same attentiveness as did their opponents, the naval staff agreed that the most favourable dates appeared to lie between September 15th and 30th when the moon would be in its last quarter.

[10]

Räder's Plans and Hopes

IN THE SPECIAL 'invasion section' set up under the super-
vision of Admiral Assmann the German naval staff worked day
and night from mid-July into September, translating into action
the many and varied instructions received through Räder and
Schniewind from the Führer's Headquarters. With marked
organizing ability and professional efficiency they went about
the unenviable task of improvising something out of nothing in
very little time, spurred on by the stern discipline of their
Commander-in-Chief, but encouraged by little else than the
scornful scepticism of the Luftwaffe and the impatient ignorance
of the Army.

At his conference with the Führer on July 25th, Räder had
set forth the Navy's principal tasks.

1. Provide and convert barges.
2. Make available the necessary personnel.
3. Prepare ports for embarkation.
4. Reconnoitre the enemy coast.
5. Clear the invasion area of mines.
6. Lay protecting minefields.
7. Set up the organization.

There were in fact two other items – one of which was dealt
with earlier at the same conference – to be added: the placing
of heavy guns between Calais and Boulogne, and the planning
of a feint attack from Norway. It was, however, the first item on
the list that, initially at all events, caused the greatest concern.

The requisitioning not merely of 'barges', but of tugs, motor
vessels, trawlers, lighters, launches and craft of all sorts up to
ships of 7,000 tons, struck a more serious blow at German
economy than any action of the British enemy could then have
done. It brought about, as Räder had warned, the almost
complete paralysis of inland water traffic, of the fishing industry

and of coastal shipping. It seriously reduced trade in the Baltic;
it endangered supplies to Norway. Moreover, with top priority
granted by the Führer, the preparing and adapting of invasion
vessels put such a strain on the limited shipyard facilities that
all naval construction, save of U-boats,[1] was brought to a
standstill; the only advantage being that naval crews – from
warships uncompleted, under repair or refitting – could be
released to man the smaller craft for which there was a severe
shortage of men trained to the sea. Altogether 24,000 men were
required for the invasion fleet, of which the Navy provided
some 4,000 and the remainder were withdrawn from merchant
ships, still further reducing the essential Baltic trade.

Taking these serious drawbacks into consideration, it is not
too much to say that, from a country whose limited maritime
capacity had suffered from the ten months' war at sea, the
effort put forth was not far short of prodigious. In little more
than six weeks the number of vessels requisitioned, to some
extent adapted and for the most part brought forward to the
coast ready for the move down to the Channel ports, was over
4,000 in all.

Among them were 170 cargo ships totalling roughly the
maximum available tonnage of 750,000; nearly 2,000 lighters
and barges collected from as far afield as the Danube as well as
from the Low Countries; some 420 tugs, including steam
trawlers capable of being used as tugs; and 1,600 smaller
motor-driven vessels of various types. Lack of time prevented
much large-scale conversion work from being carried out, nor
was it possible to construct specially designed landing craft.
The holds of the majority of the barges were provided with
concrete floors to carry the numerous army vehicles and were
fitted with interior ramps as well as with drawbridge gangways
over the bows; some were adapted to carry 3 or 4 armoured
cars, with 30 tons of additional cargo; 50 self-propelled coastal
barges were modified to carry 2 tanks each, with unloading
ramps down the side. Holds of the steam transports were fitted
to take the thousands of horses and vehicles (4,500 to an
infantry division); in a few cases hatches were enlarged and

---

[1] Eventually this construction too was much reduced.

heavier cranes fitted to speed the unloading of tanks. None of the ships could be armoured or specially protected, but some defensive armament was supplied to a number of steam transports, tugs and motor-boats, in the form of light automatic weapons (from machine guns up to 3-inch) on temporary mountings which could later be unshipped and used on land. Ready to start moving by September 1st the fleet – with an ample margin for accident, delay or loss through enemy action during assembly of between 10 and 15% – was sufficient for the requirements of the limited number of divisions in each wave, provided the total was spaced over a matter of six weeks.

In such a mixed and hurriedly collected assortment of vessels there were naturally many shortcomings and defects that could not be eliminated in the time available. Some of the defects were grave; one of the worst concerned the majority of the several hundred lighters or towed barges and lay in their dangerously low freeboard when fully loaded; so low indeed that no more than a moderate wave-height on the beam must have sufficed to swamp them. Brought to the coastal ports via the inland waterways, very few of them were given so much as a brief fairweather sea-test – perhaps wisely for the sake of the morale of those about to travel in them.

But whilst the creation of this numerous fleet was a remarkable achievement, the weak point remained. No sufficient allowance for loss through enemy action during the crossing or at the landing points was made, nor could it be made in view of the shortage of shipping. Losses inflicted upon first-echelon vessels, either outward or inward bound, were sure to have a retarding effect upon subsequent waves, until (if a substantial rate of loss were continued) the whole expedition was brought to a standstill for lack of sea transport. Yet the all-important question of how to protect the invasion fleet from enemy intervention was still as far as ever from receiving a satisfactory answer.

In the first place much appeared to depend, so the naval staff had always maintained, upon the gaining of air mastery by the Luftwaffe; but it had to be admitted that, even were it gained, for so long as the Royal Navy remained intact the safety of *Sealion* could only be assured by a number of very doubtful expedients. Although about a dozen U-boats with the necessary endurance could be spared to patrol the southern North Sea and the chops of the Channel, little was expected of them there, and no more if they were moved into the dangerous vicinity of the Dover Strait – they had achieved nothing at all at the time of Dunkirk. For the rest, apart from the small and relatively few torpedo-craft, Directive 16 provided only the proposed mine barriers on either flank of the crossing area and heavy guns firing from the French coast. Since one of the objects of the guns was to protect the minelayers, priority had evidently to be given to the setting up of the batteries.

Begun in the second half of July, the work of digging and cementing emplacements and mounting the guns in casemates was driven so rapidly forward that the first battery, of four 11-inch, was ready to fire at the beginning of August from the vicinity of Gris Nez. The second battery, of three 12-inch sited to the north of Boulogne, was ready by the middle of the month; a third, of four 15-inch to the south of Gris Nez, was due to be completed by mid-September and at about the same time a fourth would come into action with two more 11-inch between Calais and Blanc Nez. Given the advantages generally conceded to land batteries over warships, it was thought that these thirteen heavy guns, to which were added two further naval batteries of lighter calibre, might – with aircraft to direct the fire – have the value of several battleships against enemy vessels at a range of ten to fifteen miles in daylight. In conditions of bad visibility, however, or at night, against fast-moving targets for whose exact location no radar was available and no spotting by aircraft possible, it did not seem that the shooting would be very effective.

Reliance upon gunfire from the coast was stressed towards the end of August when no fewer than thirty-five heavy and medium Army batteries, plus seven heavy batteries captured from the French, were added to bring the number of guns of all calibres under naval control to the respectable total of over one hundred and fifty. And yet, surprisingly enough, it did not appear likely that this formidable artillery could succeed in denying the Dover Strait to British shipping, even in daylight. Trial shelling of merchant-ship convoys in the Channel began on August 12th, became heavy on the 22nd, and thereafter grew to be a regular feature of the passage of the strait; but although the experience was disagreeable to the crews it produced only negligible casualties to the ships – and that despite the fact that there were up to twenty-five ships in each convoy whose average speed was seldom more than 5 or 6 knots. It was scarcely to be expected that British destroyers, steaming at perhaps 20 to 30 knots through the night to intercept the sluggish *Sealion* fleet, would either be, diverted from their objective or hit save by chance.[1]

It had also been hoped that the longest-range guns would, with air co-operation, be able to put down something of a barrage[2] ahead and on either side of the invasion craft; but this fire would inevitably be confined by the limits of range to a narrow arc about the Folkestone-Dover area where, certainly inaccurate save under conditions of perfect visibility, it was unlikely to be of any real military value. With by far the greater part of the invasion area west of Folkestone lying entirely outside the range of even the heaviest guns, the naval staff could only conclude that the batteries, carefully sited and laboriously emplaced to protect the 'narrow front', would be of remarkably little use for the 'broad front' finally selected.

Now although their employment had been stipulated by Hitler at a time when he was thinking in terms of Cornwall and the Isle of Wight, he undoubtedly believed that they would be effective at Dover. Directive 16 laid down that 'heavy coastal

---

[1] Admiralty records are revealing. 'No British or foreign merchant ship was sunk by the enemy batteries throughout the war. No foreign merchant ship was damaged. Seven British merchant ships (of an aggregate tonnage of roughly 8,000) were damaged.' Admiralty figures also show that from August to December 1940 'at least 1,880 rounds were fired', and that at times as many as 200 rounds per convoy were sent over.

[2] The only occasion when this was attempted was on the night of September 10th. Destroyers of the Nore returning from a sweep of the enemy coast reported that they had been fired on by their own side. 'It seems more probable', the Dover War Diary stated, 'that (the ships) having been sighted when near the French coast the shelling was in the nature of a barrage, on the offchance of catching them.' It was wholly ineffectual.

guns must dominate and protect the entire coastal front area';
and this he had elaborated later in the Directive by ordering
that 'the largest possible number of heavy guns' – for all of
which the Navy was to be responsible – 'must be installed as
soon as possible to safeguard the crossing and to cover both
flanks against enemy interference from the sea'. Furthermore,
at the conference on July 21st, pointing to the likelihood of bad
weather and fog at the close of September, he had advocated
the 15th as the latest S-Day target date because 'after this date
co-operation between the Luftwaffe and the heavy weapons
becomes too unreliable'; and to this he had added that 'as air
co-operation is decisive, it must be regarded as the principal
factor in fixing the date'. Finally, on July 25th, he gave Räder
permission to open fire as soon as the batteries were ready, so
as 'to protect the minesweepers and to close the Dover Strait'.
Taking these various points into consideration, it is evident
that, initially, from the cross-Channel artillery bombardments
decisive results were expected.

Although these expectations were soon seen to be out of all
proportion to any possibility of fulfilment, it remained to be
discovered whether the guns could further the task of mine-
sweeping towards the English coast and, subsequently, that of
laying the mine barriers. In accordance with Hitler's decision,
action was planned to take place with the co-operation of
aircraft – and therefore in daylight. Whether Göring, by this
time fully occupied with the destruction of the British air
defences, could be relied upon to provide aircraft to spot for the
Navy was perhaps open to question; but in any case another
factor had now to be taken into careful consideration, the
lobbing of heavy shells into the Channel having become a game
at which two could play. In the second half of August various
guns newly mounted at Dover (including one of two 14-inch
manned by the Marines) began to fire back; so that the German
naval staff, if they were to claim some measure of effectiveness
for their own weapons, had perforce to admit that the Dover
guns might cause serious inconvenience to German vessels
working in the strait by day. Thus, for safety's sake, the mining

operations must be carried out, at least during the later stages when the ships would be working close to the English shore, at night – and consequently without the help of land-based gun-fire.

The initial operations – the sweeping of a channel along the Franco-Belgian coast and the laying of protective minefields some miles offshore – had been slow yet not too difficult; enemy interference and relaying of mines at sea or from the air had been relatively slight. But as the naval staff had pointed out in the memorandum of July 19th, no immunity could be counted upon when it came to sweeping mines recently laid off the English coast. And, enemy counteraction apart, the laying of the barriers outward from Calais and west of Le Havre was a matter of considerable technical complexity.

The magnetic mine had been mastered by the enemy; the new acoustic mine would not be in quantity production for some time; the moored contact mine would have to be used. But, apart from the fact that enormous quantities of these mines would be required, the Army could hardly be expected to understand the difficulties involved in their use. The notable rise and fall of the tides had to be taken into account, the more so given the relatively shallow draft of enemy patrol vessels: mines moored too near the surface would be visible at low water, moored too deep would be ineffective at high. The lack of depth in the Dover Strait, the strong tidal currents and the generally choppy sea might well cause an exceptionally large number of mines to break away from their moorings; with regular patrolling out of the question, drifting mines in the crossing area would constitute an additional danger, to be averted only by the use of additional minesweepers during the invasion; and vessels suitable for the purpose were in short supply.

Moreover, it was now evident that unless the enemy were to be permitted to know that barriers were being laid – in which case he would no doubt make every effort to sweep them up – the main operation must, for this reason too, be carried out under cover of darkness when no advantage whatever could be derived either from aircraft or from the heavy guns at Calais;

and further that even under the best conditions of weather, and of a large slice of luck in evading enemy interruption, the laying of a barrier sufficiently sturdy to render the crossing area 'completely inaccessible' to British warships was bound to take time. The British, at the beginning of the war, had required more than seven weeks to lay the Dover barrage; now, for the principal operation that had to be left to the last, the German Navy was to be allowed only ten days from the preliminary warning to S-Day. From the outset, in July, the naval staff had expressed their lack of confidence in the mine barriers as an effective means of halting the expected enemy attack upon the flanks of the invading force. They felt even less confident in September.

Only to a pitifully small extent could the flanks beyond the mine barriers be protected by German light naval forces. A flotilla of destroyers, based on Cherbourg, accompanied by a few motor torpedo-boats,[1] would shield the minelayers working out towards Selsey Bill and might just conceivably be able to ward off enemy patrol vessels during the final stages of the operation, although by so doing they would give warning of impending action. Similarly, on the Calais-Dover flank, two, perhaps three, destroyers, with a larger force of torpedo-boats would endeavour to escort the minelayers close in to the English coast. In the Dover Strait during July and August the fast motor torpedo-boats, with well-trained crews of proven efficiency, had operated successfully at night against British merchant ships passing in convoy; they might perhaps repeat their exploits against enemy minesweepers attempting to interfere with the barriers.

But the naval staff were under no illusions, or very few. The capture of the Channel ports had implied loss of control of the Dover Strait to the British; it was not to be inferred that control had thereby passed to the Germans. As time went on, evidence accumulated that the enemy was moving an average of nearly 1,000,000 tons of merchant shipping a week through the

---

[1] There were also some twenty vessels of the 'Elbing' class of small torpedo-boats. But, although completed as lately as 1937 and said to be capable of 35 knots, they do not appear to have found favour with the German Navy, since singularly little use was made of them until 1943–44.

Channel and that so far, despite the assertions of the Luftwaffe, he had lost less than 50,000 tons in the process – well under 1%. Nor did the converse hold true, namely that because the enemy could move his slow and vulnerable convoys along the English coast therefore the *Sealion* fleet would be able to cross with impunity. The two voyages were utterly different in character; the navigational difficulties of *Sealion* with its unseaworthy barges and lighters were seen more clearly than ever to be enormous; above all, the intervention of the enemy's naval forces had to be taken into account. Not the German torpedo-boats and destroyers, not the half-dozen U-boats patrolling the entrances to the Channel, not the heavy guns near Calais, not – least of all, given a night-crossing – the dive-bombers could keep British warships out of the invasion area.

Here, however, the German naval staff saw a gleam of transient hope. The enemy's naval forces did not appear, in July and even in August, to be disposed in such a way as to allow prompt intervention against the invasion fleet, and the reasons for this seemed at first to be fairly simple.

The Royal Navy's destroyer losses off Norway and Dunkirk were known to have been heavy, a fact attested by the reduction of its Atlantic convoy escorts. Increased pressure upon those convoys by the few available U-boats had sent the monthly totals of sinkings up to such heights that it seemed clear the enemy must be detaching more escorts to guard his merchant ships until such time as the fifty over-age destroyers ceded by the United States were made ready for service. Meanwhile the threatening situation in the Mediterranean, where the Italian fleet was being urged to take action, was known to be drawing off an increasing number of ships from British home waters and thus still further weakening the Home Fleet.

This fleet was rightly believed to comprise most of the modern or modernized heavy ships of the Navy, together with a number of cruisers and the remaining destroyers, but, based upon Scapa Flow and western Scottish harbours, in the view of the German naval staff its intervention against *Sealion* could scarcely be very rapid; not, at any rate, against the initial landings. Its function was clearly understood by Räder as both to guard against the intervention of supposed German heavy ships escorting an invasion fleet from Norway and to prevent, if possible, the egress of surface raiders to the Atlantic; and rumours strongly supporting both these eventualities were carefully disseminated throughout the summer. Troops and shipping were reported – sometimes actually seen – to be concentrating or embarking in various harbours from Norway to the Biscay coast; word was passed through the usual channels in neutral countries suggesting that one or other of the German heavy ships – the *Bismarck* in particular – was ready for sea; while propaganda broadcasts bluffed, double-bluffed, and occasionally dropped hints that might or might not be reliable but which, in the absence of hard news, could not be wholly ignored.

It was not expected that all of this would be swallowed hook, line and sinker by British naval intelligence; but to Räder and his associates it did appear that the Admiralty, starved of factual information, was taking some of the bait, and, accepting ·as valid the non-existent threats to Ireland, Scotland, the Shetlands and Iceland, was spreading its forces too thinly and too far. As for the main fleet at Scapa, it seemed only wise to offer something more substantial than rumour to ensure that during *Sealion*'s critical hours the heavy ships would be withheld from the southern North Sea, the cruisers and destroyers from the Channel.

To this end a simple plan was formulated. Two days before S-Day four large transports, including the liners *Bremen* and *Europa*, accompanied by the heavy cruiser *Hipper* and escorted by the 'light-cruiser squadron' – *Nürnberg, Köln, Emden* – would unite off southern Norway and steam across the North Sea, arrive in daylight somewhere between – the exact locality scarcely mattered – Aberdeen and the Tyne. Then, while the *Hipper* went north to the Iceland area, the expedition, having given the impression that it was about to attempt a landing, would retire at dusk and head back to the Skagerrak. Perhaps to make certain that if a leakage occurred the enemy should realize that something was stirring, the diversion was given the rather obvious code name of 'Autumn Voyage' (*Herbstreise*).

The weaknesses of the plan were obvious. If the ships did not steam far enough they might, under conditions of poor visibility, fail to be seen at all. If they came too close, were sighted by Coastal Command aircraft and attacked by the Fleet Air Arm of whose boldness and efficiency the German Navy had already learnt to its cost, valuable liners might be lost, the last remaining cruisers crippled or sunk, all to no purpose. And the resounding defeat of an apparent attempt to invade would do much to strengthen the will to resist in Britain.

On the other hand the feint, if successful, could have a considerable effect. Coming from the expected direction towards a vulnerable coastline, it might be mistaken for the real thing; might occupy the heavy ships from Scapa and, by drawing off light forces from the Humber and Harwich, gain for *Sealion* a measure of operational surprise. Losses might even be inflicted by the light-cruiser squadron, confusion be sown in the enemy's mind. Certainly the departure of the *Hipper* on a northerly course could not be wholly disregarded by Admiral Forbes and the Home Fleet. It was worth trying. Early in September eight more transports were detached from the Norway merchant fleet and added to the dummy invasion force.

Taken separately each of the measures planned to protect the *Sealion* crossing and its subsequent reinforcement was clearly seen by the coldly realistic naval staff to be ineffectual; yet, taken all together and in conjunction with the fact that the enemy had apparently not grasped, even during the first week in September, that the *south* coast was the objective, it did look, for perhaps no more than a few days, as if audacity might be favoured by fortune providing it were also favoured by good weather. In this sense Räder reported to Hitler on September 6th.

[11]

September 6th

ON BOTH SIDES of the narrow seas events like opposing fleets hull-down over the horizon, whose exact strength and composition cannot yet be determined, were rapidly converging to a silent decision of world importance. The shape of things to come was still far from clear to either side. But of the ten central days of crisis for Britain this Friday was the first.

On this day, after a week of heavy air attacks on southeastern England, it was recognized in Downing Street that the scales were now tipped against Fighter Command which many believed to be the keystone of Britain's defences against invasion. From the cliffs of Dover that afternoon, in suddenly perfect visibility, there were sighted, rounding Cap Gris Nez and heading west, sixty barges, tugs and steam transports – first slender indication of impending attack, not upon the east coast, but from across the choppy waters of the strait. In the evening the Home Forces were given the Preliminary Invasion Alert by their commander General Brooke: 'Attack probable within next three days.' And that night, summing up the total of intelligence received, the Admiralty directed all cruisers, destroyers and patrol craft to be kept at immediate notice until further orders.

On the previous day Hitler had signed the Directive ordering the Luftwaffe to commence the final phase of assault. Göring, at the Hague, had given instructions to Sperrle and Kesselring and now, at Beauvais, was about to inaugurate the series of day and night attacks upon London. In Berlin that afternoon the Führer summoned his Grand-Admiral to conference.

The usual personalities were present: in addition to Hitler, Generals Keitel and Jodl; the naval adjutant, Commander von Puttkamer; across the table, Räder and Schniewind. They were upon the eve of great events; four days to the first warning date, two weeks to S-Day; and to Hitler it was beginning to appear that – after all the arguments, and the weather delays, the slow fructifying of the air attack and the painful building up of the invasion fleet – the bending of England to his will before the ending of the month was beyond the power of the enemy to prevent.

Räder's report of the proceedings is the longest of all those concerning *Sealion* and, because it is more detailed, it is possible without stretching imagination too far to overhear some of the undertones and feel some of the tension. On other occasions it was frequently unnecessary for him to report details; only headings and decisions had to be mentioned; he was not writing for posterity. This time it was different; it is as though he *wanted* to be heard, to place on record his suggestions of what should be done in circumstances not yet envisaged by Hitler, so as to prove that once again the Navy had thought of it first and, from that, to gain prestige for his service.

The report begins with some account of minelaying and mine-sweeping 'in preparation for *Operation Sealion*'. Flank barrages have been laid along the Belgian coast, but in the Channel 'owing to weather conditions and the situation in air warfare, the planned operations of the minesweeping forces were delayed until now and are still greatly hampered. This is not meant as a criticism of Luftwaffe activities!'

Then, in a series of sub-sections, Norwegian defence, sub-marine warfare and auxiliary cruisers are discussed. From bases at Trondheim, Lorient and Bordeaux the operational area for submarines has been extended to the 'waters west of Scotland. It is very remunerative!' But it has to be admitted that the U-boats have suffered heavily: 'since the outbreak of war . . . 46% have been lost!' This time the exclamation mark is intended to impress the Führer so that he will 'acknowledge the contribution of the submarines in his next speech'. On the other hand, auxiliary cruisers are doing well; there are six of them at sea and 'the successes of all . . . have exceeded ex-pectations. . . . There are strong indications of concern on the part of the enemy, who is not in a position to carry out extensive search activity'.

All this must have taken time to relate and discuss, and only now does the report come to the paragraph '*Operation Sealion*'. It may well be that Räder wanted to stress the undoubtedly great advantages of U-boat and cruiser warfare so as to overshadow and diminish the unwelcome invasion scheme; and it seems possible that he heightened this effect of diminution by letting Schniewind make the progress report, since on a variety of important subjects no details are supplied. 'Information is given on transport space, the assembly thereof, clearing of the harbours, fuel supplies, provision of personnel, minesweeping and minelaying. . . .' It all sounds rather tediously technical.

Abruptly: 'Relevant charts are shown.' A terse announcement, yet one can almost hear the crackle of stiff paper. Probably there were other sounds, of a general movement and shifting of chairs as Hitler stood up and, leaning forward, pressed his palms upon the table to stare intently at the maps – a favourite attitude. Now at last, he must have examined attentively that seventy-mile stretch of Kent and Sussex coastline upon which his troops were so soon to be thrown, whilst Räder or Schniewind talked again of tidal currents and rocky shoals and the dangers of an onshore wind in an open roadstead. Perhaps he saw now how wide was the gap 'Alderney to Portland' which, in Directive 16, he had ordered to be closed with mine-barriers so as to make the *Sealion* flank 'completely inaccessible'.

Then came Räder's summing-up: 'If air supremacy is increasingly established it will be possible to meet the new deadline. . . .' The 'deadline' was for the assembly of the steam transports, 'new' because it was only three days since the order had been issued (September 3rd) by Keitel from Supreme Headquarters, fixing the earliest day for the sailing of the invasion fleet at September 20th.

Paragraph 3 of the order had stated: 'Final commands will be given at the latest on S-Day minus 3 at noon' – therefore on September 17th. But doubts had been expressed of the possibility of assembling the transports in their respective harbours before the 19th, which would be cutting it very fine for embarkation on the 20th. Now, however, the latest reports suggested that, after all, the vessels essential for the first wave would all be assembled by the 15th; and *Sealion* could sail on the 20th.

Even so, Räder found it necessary to add a grim warning that seemed to pour cold sea-water upon the whole scheme. 'The crossing itself will be very difficult. The Army cannot rely on being able to keep the divisions together.'

Hitler was not one to care for the hardships of his troops or for the discomfort of his Generals; but to a man who blended an artistic temperament with constitutional fear of the sea the mental picture of storm-tossed barges ploughing slowly through the night, losing touch, becoming scattered, some swamped, the remainder disgorging their cargo of seasick soldiers into the booming surf of an unfamiliar shore, must have appeared unaesthetic if not forbidding. So that it seems permissible to suppose that at this point he interjected a sharp query: Is the project feasible or not? For, in the next paragraph of the report, Räder commits himself to a positive declaration.

'The execution of *Operation Sealion* appears possible. . . .' At last, an encouraging phrase! Perhaps something of Hitler's bold recklessness gripped him, for he had never gone so far hitherto. And even now he quickly covers himself with several weighty conditionals: '. . . appears possible if attended by favourable circumstances regarding air supremacy, weather, etcetera.'

This 'etcetera' in the report is masterly. It covers the whole distasteful topic of British command of the sea, which is not otherwise mentioned. Perhaps Räder knocked on wood to bid the unwelcome spectre avaunt; he had little else with which to make it vanish. Only the *Herbstreise*.

'In the north a diversionary manoeuvre (a dummy landing) is planned with four large steamers from the German Bight, ten steamers from the Norwegian area, and escort forces. The *Hipper* is to operate in the Iceland area, in order to relieve the dummy landing operation.'

The dummy was gaining in importance. Two more ships had been added to it.

And that was all, as far as *Sealion* was directly concerned. It appears probable that Hitler made some further remark;

perhaps he took up the question of 'air supremacy' and explained the expected result of the new air assault: that the British collapse would make the *Sealion* crossing unnecessary. Because, in the report's third section, Räder suddenly asks: 'What are the Führer's political and military directives if *Operation Sealion* does not take place?' And follows up with the hope that production may be re-established in German industry, 'through the return of personnel and of the steamers, other vessels and barges'.

The report then sets forth the naval staff's views on various promising operations in the Mediterranean area 'in addition to, or instead of, *Operation Sealion*', the principal and most important objective being Gibraltar, for the capture of which preparations 'must be begun at once so that they are completed before the U.S.A. steps in'. It must have been satisfying to be able to record that: 'The Führer gives orders to this effect.'

The problem presented by the United States was examined further, for it was correctly estimated at the conference that the fall or conquest of Britain would not entail the immediate submission of the rest of the world. 'The British Empire is not expected to collapse, owing to the peculiar innate force of the political objectives embodied in the conception of the Commonwealth of Nations.' America with Canada might take over the leadership of the Anglo-Saxon empire and continue the fight; already the handing over of the fifty destroyers was 'an openly hostile act against Germany'; soon the United States might be expected to occupy the Spanish and Portuguese Atlantic islands; worse still, they might move into the British and French possessions in West Africa. 'The Commander-in-Chief Navy stresses once again the extreme importance of Dakar for Germany in this war.' To which the Führer added that the occupation of the Canary Islands by the Luftwaffe would be 'both expedient and feasible'.

Thereafter, for lack of topics, the world-political discussion seems to have petered out, and the conference sat back to listen in respectful silence to the Führer's answer to a question put by Räder 'regarding treatment of occupied northern areas of Sweden and Finland'.

There should be, Hitler opined, a North Germanic Union 'in which the individual members have a certain sovereignty' with diplomatic representation and German-trained forces, but otherwise they should be 'both politically and economically closely connected with Germany. These are the views of Quisling, whose standpoint the Führer recognizes to be the correct one . . . the Navy alone, moreover, held these views quite rightly from the very first.'

With that, after brief mention of the necessity for 'ruthless submarine warfare', the conference came to an end, and Räder went away evidently well pleased with the pat on the back for his complicity in the Norway affair.

But when he talked it over with Schniewind in the office at the Ministry of Marine, it must have been with very mixed feelings that they read through the conference notes. For all the broad hints at the possibility of *Sealion* not taking place, for all the tempting bait of Gibraltar and the Canary Isles, the red herring of American intervention in West Africa, it was plain as a pikestaff that the Führer's orders for invasion still stood. Postponement? It was the attack on Russia that had been postponed; the Soviet Union had not been so much as mentioned at the conference. The season was in any case too far advanced; the recent despatch of 10 divisions to Poland, of 2 armoured divisions to the Roumanian frontier was no more than wise insurance against a possible stab in the back from Russia whilst England was being finished off. But the seaborne invasion was very much on.

Hitler had issued his commands to the Army; it was ready, trained and, despite grumbles at the narrowness of the front, amply confident. He had given the order for the final phase of the air assault; Göring had raised his Marshal's baton, Sperrle and Kesselring were eager to go. He had listened to the Commander-in-Chief Navy, had examined the plans in detail, had heard the Grand-Admiral say that '*Operation Sealion* appears possible'. No further argument was admissible.

Sealion would be launched when the Führer gave the word, probably on the 20th. Just possibly it would be retarded to the

23rd, the Navy's optimum date, which would bring the warning date to the 13th and give everyone a little more time to assemble the ships and, perhaps, to guard against enemy naval interference if by any evil chance 'etcetera' got wind of the plan.

The naval staff watched the weather reports with anxiety. Much depended upon them; if the weather broke in good time, there could be a postponement and no harm done; if too late, if a storm blew up without so much as twenty-four hours' warning, *Sealion*, as once the Armada, might be scattered and wrecked. On the 7th it was fine.

[12]

Wrong Target

I

IT WOULD BE an injustice to say of the German naval staff at this time that they were as much in the dark about air power as the army staff about sea power. Senior naval officers, who from the earliest days of flying had appreciated the value of the air arm as an extension of naval power, had for years fought a losing battle against the domination of the Luftwaffe whose officers were drawn almost exclusively from an Army ignorant, for the most part, of the very element upon which maritime affairs are conducted. Starved by Göring's ambition, and Luftwaffe jealousy, of those naval aircraft, torpedo-bombers, minelayers and the like, with which they might well have developed a deadlier attack upon the British fleets, it had been with a sense of frustration that the naval staff had noted the mighty effects of air bombing in swiftly victorious campaigns. Air attacks on Warsaw had ended Polish resistance; a single devastating raid on Rotterdam had paralysed the Dutch; the threat of similar destruction had caused the French to abandon Paris. Then, too, they had observed (to their sorrow) the sinking of the *Königsberg* at Bergen; had seen the Luftwaffe dive-bombers retaliate by pulverising British destroyers off Dunkirk and punishing the convoys off Dover. It was hard not to believe in the omnipotence of the air weapon, harder still not to be able to command its employment in connection with *Sealion*.

The naval staff did not, as is sometimes suggested, 'pass the buck' to Göring; it was not theirs to pass. The Commander-in-Chief of the Luftwaffe, ranking high in the Nazi hierarchy, was a law unto himself. Only Hitler stood above him, and Hitler supported his plans and policy. In conference Räder might express his reasoned views, and note with satisfaction: 'The Führer agrees'; once Göring had obtained a written order there was nothing the Grand-Admiral could do, save cautiously to point out at the next conference that the order had not been wholly fulfilled. But against Luftwaffe strategy early in September he had little to say. It was, in the main, what he himself had advocated from the start.

'For a speedy termination of the war with Britain', he had told Hitler on July 11th, 'the impact of the war must be forcibly brought home to the British public itself.' This, he suggested, required heavy air attacks to be made on 'the great mass of people who cannot be evacuated' in the larger towns and especially in London. The series of attacks begun on September 7th were, therefore, in general accordance with his own considered opinion of the best method of subduing Britain.

Nor, as the Luftwaffe reports came in on the 8th, did the naval staff find any immediate cause for complaint. There could be no doubt in their minds that a very considerable success had been scored: the defences of London had been penetrated in broad daylight and, despite the utmost efforts of the enemy fighters, 300 tons of bombs and many thousands of incendiaries had been dropped in the space of one and a half hours upon the dock area on either side of the Thames. Nearly 1,000 German aircraft had been engaged; their losses had been scarcely 4%. That same night, guided by the pulsating glow of the immense fires started in daytime, some 250 bombers had returned to the attack and this time they had suffered no loss at all. No enemy fighters intercepted; few anti-aircraft guns opened up, and those few only after nine o'clock. Another 300 tons of high explosives were dropped, together with more than 400 canisters of incendiaries.

In at least one way this looked like the beginning of the end for Britain. Added to the damage already done, by day on the 5th, by night on the 5th and 6th, to Tilbury docks and the Thameshaven oil installations, the havoc now wrought upon the supply organization of the capital seemed to presage speedy victory: '40% of the imports', Räder had told Hitler in July, 'come through the Port of London.' That port was now a blazing wreck.

And yet, in the opinion of the naval staff, something was lacking. It was not a failure to keep to the time-table. The arbitary period of approximately one month for the reduction of the enemy air forces and the destruction of his aircraft reserves and factories had been extended by bad weather as much as by the enemy's fierce resistance, but not unduly extended. There had been some miscalculation, evidently; an under-estimate of British fighter strength, an over-estimate of enemy losses; but it made little difference to the foreseeable result and, given that *Sealion* could not sail before mid-September, it scarcely affected the schedule. Already the enemy's resistance was weakening; his losses, whatever the true figures, were now far higher than he could afford, whilst those of the Luftwaffe, though heavy at times, were still easily bearable for so great a result.

Begun on August 15th the air attack now merging into the bombing assault on the capital would surely achieve, by September 15th, the requisite degree of air mastery. Of that the Luftwaffe was positive; only further bad weather could upset the plan. Even now, attacked everywhere, the enemy was being·compelled to throw in his last reserves of pilots and aircraft to the defence of London, upon which – in the German air staff's view – the maximum effort must continue to be directed to the exclusion of all other objectives.

It was this that caused the naval staff a swiftly growing uneasiness. The Luftwaffe seemed to be losing sight of the central purpose, according to the Führer's Directives, of all the air attacks: the furthering of the *Sealion* operations, both naval and military. True, the total devastation of a large part of London, and the concurrent elimination of its fighter defences, might well in due course produce a British collapse; but this probability, however desirable in itself, was relatively remote compared to the near-certainty of *Sealion* being ordered within a day or two. When, despite bad weather on the 8th and 9th, which reduced the scale of attack and to that extent upset the time-table, the Luftwaffe continued to concentrate against the capital, it became clear that there would scarcely be time for attacks urgently needed elsewhere to become effective. The warning date was less than two days off, or at best, for the optimum S-Day, but four days away. *Sealion* objectives, Räder could only conclude, were being deliberately neglected.

Had they been wholly neglected during the first phases of the air battle his path would have been more direct, though not necessarily smoother. He could have protested to Hitler, have pointed out that the Führer's own orders were not being obeyed. It was the fact that they were not being flagrantly disobeyed that made things difficult.

It had been as early as June 20th that he had called the Führer's attention 'to the necessity of starting vigorous air attacks on British bases in order to destroy ships under construction or repair'; to which he had added, on July 11th, 'air attacks on convoys, and heavy air attacks on her (Britain's) main centres, Liverpool, for instance'. And in some measure all these things had been done.

The trouble was that, largely because of the lack of precise orders in Directive 16, they had not been done sufficiently or effectively enough. During the first phase, from mid-July to early August, quite a number of 'vigorous air attacks' had been carried out both on convoys and on British harbours and naval bases along the south coast. Dover, Portsmouth, Portland, Plymouth had all been bombed more than once; but save in the case of Dover, whence the destroyers had been withdrawn, the effect had been far from conclusive. To obtain a result of enduring value for *Sealion* heavier and more persistent attacks would be necessary. With the opening of the intensified air war in mid-August the naval staff had the right to expect that, although the destruction of the British Air Force must be the Luftwaffe's first objective, a more serious effort would be directed to *Sealion* targets.

And so, to some extent, it was; but once again, in Directive 17[1] as in 16, Hitler's orders were too vague.

After a spell of bad weather, from August 18th to 23rd, the attacks on naval objectives were resumed, on the afternoon of the 24th, with a raid by fifty bombers on Portsmouth where extensive damage was done to both town and dockyard. That

[1] See Appendix A.

night Plymouth was attacked and, among other ports, Cardiff,
Swansea and Hull. Bombs were also dropped on Birmingham,
Leeds, the Bomber Command airfield at Driffield and, for the
first time since 1918, on London. Two days later another, less
successful attack was made on Portsmouth and again, that
night, on Plymouth. Other raids followed during the last days
of the month on Portsmouth and Portland, but they were on a
small scale and, whatever the Luftwaffe might claim, not very
effective. Much more was needed; the naval staff could only
hope that they would get it.

Meanwhile, on the night of August 28th and on the three
following nights, a series of heavy attacks was made on the
Liverpool district where 70% of the air-crews claimed to have
reached the target area. An average of more than 155 bombers
took part each night, dropping nearly 115 tons of bombs on
each raid, so that it was only natural to suppose that heavy
damage had been inflicted. In any event the naval staff could
hardly disagree with the policy of concentrating upon the
Mersey area, since Liverpool had been one of the objectives
specifically mentioned by Räder, and their approval was made
plain by the co-operation in the attacks of a number of naval
Focke-Wulf *Kondors* drawn from units organized for co-operation
in the U-boat war and trained for attacks on merchant shipping. Nevertheless, the onslaught, in fact no more than partially
successful, could only be regarded as a part, though an important one, of the general and longer-term war against
Britain; except for the fact that Liverpool and Birkenhead were
naval repair and construction bases, it contributed little to the
prospects of *Sealion*, for which further sustained assaults in the
south and south-east were more than ever necessary. They
were expected early in September.

But the first week of the month found the Luftwaffe engaged
in a carefully calculated attempt to have done with the
remaining enemy fighters by wrecking both their ground
organization and their aircraft factories; and judging from even
the most conservative estimates it was apparent that the
German airmen were meeting with a considerable measure of
success. Enemy strength was dwindling, fewer bombers were

being intercepted before reaching their objectives, the defences were being swamped. All of which might make it seem strange to the naval staff that, with vast fleets of German bombers swarming over Kent, the Medway and the Thames estuary, no serious efforts were being made to destroy the naval bases at Sheerness and Harwich where some of the enemy's light forces now appeared to be concentrated. But the choice of targets and the scale and timing of attacks were the prerogative of the air staff who could always claim that Hitler's orders were being carried out in the general sense of his successive ambiguous Directives.

Thus, from phase to phase, from day to day and from one attack to another, the naval staff bridled their impatience and waited for the Luftwaffe to turn with maximum strength to objectives more directly concerned with *Sealion*. It may be that in July Räder had not insisted enough upon the necessity of those 'vigorous attacks' on British naval bases; and later on he said remarkably little about them at the various conferences with Hitler, although he seldom missed a chance of reiterating that 'complete air mastery' was essential to invasion. Caution may have counselled him to play the waiting game, to let Göring have his head, to see whether he would not, after all and within the time limit, accomplish the downfall of Britain. If he failed, and meanwhile had not seriously damaged the British fleet, postponement of the seaborne operation would be not so much necessary as inevitable.

By the naval staff it was noted, when the final assault began on September 7th, that the Luftwaffe intended at the Führer's command 'to bring about the complete destruction of London's harbours, docks, industries and supplies by means of continuous air attacks, and so hasten the decision'. But, although it was appreciated that these attacks would absorb a large part of the Luftwaffe's effort, it was still supposed that enemy naval installations and coastal objectives connected with *Sealion* would receive a greater share of attention than hitherto. When, however, the reports came in on the 8th and it was seen that little more than token raids had been made on Portsmouth and Southampton, and that nothing at all was being done in the

Dover area or on the south-east coast; when, moreover, on the same day the Luftwaffe issued a triumphant statement declaring that the all-absorbing attacks on London would be continued 'until the destruction of harbours, supplies and power installations is complete'; the naval staff saw the light at last. The Luftwaffe – Göring, Kesselring, Sperrle and the air staff – had no intention whatever of turning their main strength to assisting the seaborne invasion. They were, with dangerous over-confidence in German air power, contemptuously neglecting British sea power.

To the naval staff wisdom came too late for the prospering of *Sealion*. The Army might believe that the Luftwaffe was doing, in the well-remembered words of Directive 16, 'the work of the artillery'. To the Navy it seemed as if, towards zero-hour in a land battle, the 'artillery' was ranging the back areas hoping for a knock-out blow on the enemy headquarters and forgetting altogether the front-line defences and the forces massed for counter-attack on the flank.

Over London, Göring might or might not be drawing near to strategic victory. As far as the *Sealion* crossing was concerned, he was, with Hitler's approval, hitting at the wrong target. 'It is desirable that the English fleets should be pinned down shortly before the crossing.' To achieve the 'desirable' nothing was done.

II

Much was said and written that summer about air 'superiority', air 'ascendancy', air 'supremacy', air 'mastery', and yet neither side understood at the time just how much or how little, it was necessary to the first stages of the invasion plan.

In the naval staff's memorandum of July 19th it was stated that 'the gaining of air supremacy is vital to the possibility of assembling the requisite naval forces and shipping in the relatively restricted area of embarkation', and this was underlined on the 21st by Hitler who, on Räder's advice, laid down as the first of the prerequisites for invasion 'complete mastery of the air'. On the 25th, in conference with Hitler, Räder mentioned it again, stressing that the gaining of air superiority was a necessity 'in order to carry out preparations'.

It is clear, then, that at the start it was thought impossible to assemble and launch the invasion fleet unless all organized forces of enemy aircraft had been driven from the skies over Continental Europe and the Channel. It was not to be expected that, with England still unconquered and still, by S-Day, not wholly subdued by air attack, there would be no aircraft at all to make a last desperate fight over Britain; the important thing was that there should be no coherent force capable of interfering with any of the invasion preparations.

As time went on, however, the naval staff came to realize – although they did not say so openly, no doubt lest the Luftwaffe should be encouraged to take things easy – that this mastery of their own skies did not need to be absolute. They had before them the example of the British convoys: if the British, despite every effort of the dive-bombers, could continue to pass something like 1,000,000 tons of shipping up and down the Channel every week, then surely the German Navy could manage to assemble within a fortnight a mere 700,000 tons, protected during the coastal journey by countless German fighters and menaced only by a relatively small force of British bombers. It was not perhaps quite so simple as that; yet even in September when, against the Luftwaffe's sanguine claim of approaching air victory, the naval staff were grumbling that the British bomber force was still 'at full operational strength', they had to admit that its activities were causing 'no decisive hindrance' to the movement of German transports. The *Sealion* fleet could, it appeared, be made ready *without* 'complete mastery of the air'.

Upon the Army divisions, once landed in England, air supremacy would obviously confer tremendous advantages and the converse serious, but not necessarily disastrous risks. Provided that the Luftwaffe gave them support and did the 'work of the artillery', and that the Navy ferried over the requisite anti-aircraft guns, they were not unduly worried about the opposition to be expected from enemy air forces already small and steadily weakening. After all, they had experienced considerable air opposition in France and had driven through easily enough in spite of it. With German fighters at least the equal in quality and vastly superior in quantity, sufficient air superiority seemed assured; it was all they needed. They were much more concerned about the speed with which the Navy could deliver supplies and reinforcements for the second echelon.

The Luftwaffe saw the whole struggle against Britain in a very different light. From the outset Göring had scarcely regarded it as a struggle at all. There would be some resistance of course, the English were stubborn combatants and they possessed some good fighter aircraft; but the German fighters were invincible, the bombers irresistible. Both had proved their worth in peace and war; the mere fact of their existence had won the day at Munich; the threat of action at Prague had caused the surrender of Czechoslovakia; in three swiftly decisive campaigns they had contributed powerfully to victory. Nothing could withstand them. Air power was everything and Germany wielded it; it had superseded sea power, it dominated land power, it could exert world political power.

In the Führer's Directive 17 the Luftwaffe was ordered 'to overcome the English air forces in the shortest possible time'. In the air staff's view it would not take long. A few days to reduce the fighters and their organization, a couple of weeks to wreck the remaining airfields and the aircraft factories, at most two more to devastate the main supply centres by day and by night; allowing for bad weather, in a month it would be over. *Sealion* was unnecessary, save for occupation purposes. Mastery in the air meant mastery of all Britain.

At times as the battle progressed Göring and his Generals appeared to be standing on their heads and, seeing the picture upside down, transposing the figures for their own and the enemy's losses; at others to be possessed of a certain *Looking-glass* logic, as when the bombers were ordered not to attack the all-important radar towers again because previous attacks had been unsuccessful. And yet, gradually and through sheer weight of numbers – not through superior skill, still less through greater

gallantry – they achieved a considerable measure of success.
Even the German naval staff, soberly examining the Luftwaffe's
claims and far from wishing to indulge in flattery, were ready
to agree on September 10th that 'the preparatory attacks of the
Luftwaffe have achieved a perceptible weakening of enemy
fighter defence, so that it can be taken for granted that the
German forces have a considerable fighter superiority over the
English area'.

It was in fact the beginning of a tactical success which,
rightly applied, might have done much to improve *Sealion's*
chances. But Göring and the air Generals, wrongly discerning
the approach of strategic victory, chased after it with unerring
misjudgment of the military situation as a whole, turning their
backs upon the invasion plan which was supposed to be the
main object of the exercise and the principal reason for seeking
air supremacy at all at this juncture. On the analogy of a land
battle, they had attacked the centre – Fighter Command – and
despite determined resistance and heavy losses had made good
progress, almost disrupting the defence. To turn the wavering
into a rout, they had then smashed at the easier flank – the
industrial and population centres, the factories and docks of
London – and, attacking by night, suffered no loss whilst
inflicting immense damage. That on this flank they would in
the long run meet with defeat, not by the Royal Air Force
which could take no part in the night battle, but by the will to
resist of the British people inspired by Churchill, was something
beyond their limited vision. But meanwhile, with their strength
fully deployed, they had nothing to spare for the other flank –
the enemy's naval concentrations, Räder's 'etcetera'.

In the naval staff's report of September 10th it was stated:
'It is of decisive importance for the judgment of the situation
that no claim can be made to the destruction of the enemy air
force over southern England and the Channel area.' The stipulated air mastery, however near, had not yet been achieved, and
there was but one day left before the warning date.

It had nevertheless become evident, by the 6th, that the
Luftwaffe had established superiority by day and, by the 7th,

supremacy at night; whilst the enemy, almost powerless to hit back by day, was establishing a measure of superiority over the Channel ports by night, albeit with small forces whose maximum effort was likely to remain indecisive. As to *Sealion* it seemed quite plain that there was now neither time nor intention to 'pin down' the British fleets.

For Räder and the naval staff it had become vitally important to know what were their minimum requirements from the Luftwaffe if *Sealion* were to sail at all. The safeguarding conditions under which the expedition might be launched with some reasonable hope of success could be summarized thus:

1. *Herbstreise*, the 'dummy landing', and *Hipper* to Iceland.
2. Minesweeping up to the English coast.
3. Minelaying on either flank of the crossing area.
4. Protection by light naval forces.
5. Heavy gun barrage.
6. Local surprise.
7. Favourable weather.

For the first, 'complete air mastery' was unnecessary. Indeed it was highly desirable that enemy patrolling aircraft should be allowed to continue their work undisturbed, so that the brief appearance of the dummy force might be promptly and certainly reported during S-Day minus 1 and the British naval forces drawn off during the night of the crossing. The decoy duck would be no decoy at all unless it was seen before it retired.

As regards points 2 to 6: the final stages of both minesweeping and laying were to be carried out, during the ten days' warning period, *at night*. If the enemy countered by sweeping and relaying he too would do it *by night*. The crossing itself, for which the very limited amount of naval protection available was necessary, was to be made *during the hours of darkness* – when the heavy guns, if they fired at all, could not be relied upon for accuracy. Since the enemy, according to the scanty intelligence reports, still appeared to expect a landing north of the Thames estuary, tactical surprise on the south coast could perhaps still be maintained, even after the assault landing, by moving the second echelon reinforcement ships from Antwerp and Rotterdam *by night*.

To none of these nocturnal operations could the Luftwaffe bring any direct assistance. But, conversely, the Royal Air Force could do nothing to stop them. Fighter Command could not operate at night; Bomber Command, with too few aircraft and bombs of insufficient power, could not inflict decisive damage upon the invasion fleet before it sailed. To the launching of *Sealion* the total destruction of the enemy's air forces was not essential.

One target existed, and only one, whose destruction was a matter of life or death to the invasion plan. The naval staff had foreseen it from the start – from the start of the war – but had been overborne by the air-power enthusiasts asserting that sea power was a thing of the past. They saw it now; but, overawed by Hitler, impressed in spite of themselves by Göring's massive assault on London, they failed to stress the need for immediate action in accordance with the Directives. Instead of a demand, they made a tactful understatement.

'It would be more in the sense of the planned preparation for *Operation Sealion*', they hinted reproachfully on September 10th, 'if the Luftwaffe would now concentrate less on London and more on Portsmouth and Dover, and on the naval forces in and near the operation area, in order to wipe out any possible threat from the enemy. . . .'

It was being said in England – it was to be repeated more emphatically later on – that Göring had begun his assault on London too soon. It seems more realistic to say that he started too late. Had he thrown everything in against the capital early in August he would have achieved as much as in September for no greater loss – by night, at all events – and, since it would have become clear by the end of the month (as in fact it became clear by October) that he was not going to obtain the immediate surrender of Britain, there would still have been time to divert his main effort to those two targets, only a few miles away at

Harwich and Sheerness, whose destruction offered *Sealion* its
only chance of success.

Even after the 10th there might have been time; though with
bad weather intervening the period to S-Day would have been
all too short for anything approaching decisive action against
the numerous and far-spread British fleets. But no one gave the
order, and not even Räder felt like remonstrating with Hitler
just then.

'The Naval War Staff', his staff reported (September 10th),
'does not consider it suitable to approach the Luftwaffe or the
Führer now with such demands, because the Führer looks upon
a large-scale attack on London as being possibly decisive, since
a systematic and long-drawn-out bombardment of London may
produce an attitude in the enemy which will make the *Sealion*
operation completely unnecessary.'

In a sense this belief of Hitler's suited Räder well enough.
The only enemy 'attitude' which could render *Sealion* 'completely unnecessary' must be total collapse. Then, with resistance at an end, a token force might steam triumphantly up the
Thames estuary to land the occupation troops; and British
warships might cross the North Sea to offer their surrender in
German ports as once the German Fleet had crossed to surrender in the Firth of Forth. 'The German ensign will be
lowered at sunset and will not be hoisted again.' For Beatty's
order, sweet revenge!

But what if the collapse did *not* ensue within the next few days,
if the foreshadowed panic, chaos, revolution and surrender did
not materialize at once? What if Göring should claim that,
with 'complete air mastery' in the night skies and 'supremacy'
nearly won by day, with London in ruins and the defences
wrecked, the time was ripe for *Sealion* to give the *coup de grâce*?
What then? Were Brauchitsch and Halder to insist, the Supreme
Command might well agree and so advise the Führer. If Hitler
gave the order, none would dare to protest. *Sealion* would sail
to its doom.

For one thing was certain. Whatever had been accomplished
over England, in the skies or upon the battered towns, the
German air weapon had not eliminated British command of

the sea. It had not even challenged it. The Royal Navy was
intact and alert. Unless and until it was eliminated the old
Tirpitz dictum still rang true: 'Against England the main front
is the sea front.'

That front Räder now watched with increasing anxiety.

[13]

News from Paris

IT WAS NOT arrogance alone that brought the conquerors in
large numbers to Paris that summer, that caused the best hotels
to be taken over and the staffs of many headquarters to settle
in as solidly as though the city were to become a permanent
branch office of Berlin. The French capital was still the great
centre of road, rail and river transport and of telecommunica-
tions. From it not only could France be controlled, operations
against Britain could also be directed. It was convenient; it was
central; it was also safe.

For one thing at least was certain: whatever stern measures
the British might feel compelled to take against the French
fleet to prevent its falling into German hands, they would never
bomb the centre of Paris. Secure in this knowledge, Admiral
Saalwächter set up in the Avenue Hoche the headquarters of
Naval Group West, responsible for maritime organization from
the Narrow Seas to the Spanish frontier.

For the victors life had an agreeable sparkle that summer in
Paris; with the conquest of France behind them, the conquest
of Britain ahead, the Army invincible and the Luftwaffe
supreme, there was scarcely a cloud upon the horizon. So that
perhaps it was only the naval staff who could appreciate what
a stormy voyage lay ahead if England were not brought down
that year, could remember what they had said a year ago: that
the war was lost on the day Britain had declared it. Now the
sun shone and all seemed well with the German cause, but
what might not happen if Britain fought on, was allowed to
gain time and strength? The future was shadowy. Fortunately
for their peace of mind, there was urgent work to be done; they
applied themselves to it diligently.

Their tasks were many and widespread. With the Atlantic
seaboard within their purlieu the Biscay ports yielded merchant

shipping, to be grouped so as to give colour to the carefully concocted rumours of planned attacks on Cornwall, Ireland or the Hebrides; yielded too their naval bases, at Brest and Lorient, to be organized for the reception of German warships. U-boats came in, were refuelled and supplied, and set forth again to prey upon the trade routes. Coastal defences were manned, anti-aircraft units moved up. Even before the *Sealion* Directive was issued repairs were begun in the Channel ports, of which Dunkirk, Calais and Boulogne had all been extensively damaged. Towards the end of June, Boulogne and Cherbourg were designated as bases for motor torpedo-boats, Brest for the U-boats.

With the development of the invasion plan the net of organization was spread wider, to draw in from the waterways of France and the Low Countries the large numbers of barges and lighters, to supervise their speedy adaptation – and the generous scale of compensation to their owners – and to direct their assembly upon the coast. Presently the motor torpedo-boats and minesweepers were received into the area, the former to join in the night attacks on Channel convoys, the latter to start an experimental clearing of the enemy's mines in the Dover Strait.

Signals to Berlin on these and other matters, ranging from weather reports to casualties caused by enemy action, were detailed and frequent. Towards the end of August the information they included concerning the activities of enemy warships and aircraft assumed considerable importance to Räder and his staff. By September, with the transports assembling in the Channel ports, their forecasts of deadlier enemy counteraction had become of great consequence to the fate of the entire expedition.

In the latter half of that month of August it became evident to the staff in Berlin that German naval strategy had suffered a secret but serious setback. Already air reconnaissance of British bases, hitherto valuable and accurate, had been much reduced, in part due to increased British counter-measures, in part to the frequent spells of poor visibility as well as to the

Luftwaffe's lack of co-operation. Now all at once the German Navy found that it had lost, not its eyesight, but its very acute sense of hearing. The Admiralty had changed the Royal Navy's codes and cyphers.

It was a long story. During the First World War, with wireless communication still in its infancy, the Royal Navy had developed an interception service which, with remarkable accuracy, had given early warning of every important move of the High Seas Fleet. After the war, with that fleet safely surrendered and for the most part at the bottom of Scapa Flow, there had appeared to be no further reason for secrecy, and a large amount of information, technical as well as general, was handed out in memoirs and histories. It was only natural therefore that when Germany began to rebuild her Navy the creation of a similar but, given immense technical progress over the years, superior service should be regarded as of capital importance. The task, undertaken with German thoroughness, was driven forward with such assiduity that by the outbreak of war the naval staff could not only check the disposition and movements of British warships, but, helped by a smart piece of intelligence work, could also read their signals. The most secret Admiralty code was broken.

It had accounted for a great deal during the first eleven months of war. For the uncanny ease with which surface raiders had eluded the Home Fleet; for the relative immunity from interception of German heavy ships off Norway; for certain surprise attacks on British warships; for the sinking of six submarines in the Skagerrak area between June and August. To more than one British commander it had seemed that, whereas they seldom knew of the whereabouts of the enemy's ships, the enemy always knew everything about theirs. A more temperamental race might well have suspected treachery.

At long last the Admiralty tumbled to the truth. On August 20th the codes and cyphers were abruptly changed. And with the change one of the main props of German operational planning was knocked away. Worse than that: the naval staff had for so long been able to depend upon sure knowledge of British operations and intentions that they had come to take this knowledge for granted. It had exerted decisive influence upon the Norway plans and, from the success of that campaign, it had encouraged the planning of invasion. Now, within a month of *Sealion's* sailing, the great advantage had been taken from them. Of the strength and disposition of the majority of British warships in home waters they had no longer any certain knowledge. A mute wall of fog had descended over the harbours and anchorages of Britain.

At this late hour the work must be started all over again. Patrols and reconnaissance – surface, underwater, air – must search and discover, find out swiftly what forces were being concentrated upon the *Sealion* flanks. Along the south and south-eastern seaboard of England the main tasks lay within the orbit of Naval Group West.

In Berlin the naval staff read with increasing attention the news from Paris. It was not encouraging.

[14]

Ten Nights to Decision: I

SEPTEMBER 6TH – 10TH

AT HALF-PAST TEN in the evening of that same Friday on which Räder had told the Führer that *Sealion* '*appears possible if*——', the Admiralty signal brought all cruisers, destroyers and small craft to 'immediate notice'. Darkness had fallen and as usual patrols from the Nore, Dover and Portsmouth were already at sea, preceded by destroyers. At 11 p.m. four MTBs (motor torpedo-boats) followed as the watch on the enemy coast across the narrow seas was intensified. Invasion was not expected immediately, not on the 6th. Although the alert issued to the Royal Air Force stated that it was 'imminent, and probable within 12 hours', by the Admiralty it was now estimated that the tide would serve best between the 8th and the 10th. But it was only wise to see what the enemy was up to and to be ready, if he showed signs of a desire to come forward, to meet him more than half-way.

The moon had already set when the MTBs and destroyers closed the Franco-Belgian coast. It was a dark night, with a gusty breeze and only moderate visibility, but bearings were not hard to take. High above the low-lying shore bursting shells sparked intermittently; on land, in the immediate vicinity of the ports, the pallid gleam of flares contrasted with the orange glow of spreading fires and the rumble of gunfire was punctuated by the thud of exploding bombs. A lively scene, reminiscent of that Saint George's Day in 1918 when the blockships had headed in towards Zeebrugge and Ostend. . . . A different class of vessel lay in Ostend harbour now: lighters and barges in growing numbers. Ten days ago there had been none; now, as air reconnaissance had shown, there were over 200. And that very day the concentration of 60 vessels, tugs and small coasters had been sighted off Calais: were they already laden with troops and supplies? What was the enemy preparing? To most men it seemed certain that he would bring, if not some new and fearful weapon to make up for his weakness at sea, at least special landing craft and tank-carrying ferries. But where and when would he strike? There was no sign yet of any forward movement. The MTBs ran on down the French coast; they encountered no enemy, but the enemy did not fail to note their passing.

Farther back, in mid-Channel, the small ships cruised – the sloops, the gunboats, the minesweeping trawlers – ready both to give warning and to attack. Three nights previously a fishing vessel, escorted by two German minesweepers, had sneaked over from Le Touquet to land four luckless spies between Dungeness and Hythe. To make sure that no such isolated vessels ever succeeded in making a crossing was next to impossible. That an assembly of hundreds of lighters, barges, tugs and trawlers, nosing their slow and uncertain way on a front of seventy miles would not be challenged on passage, even supposing their departure to have gone unreported, was scarcely imaginable. The patrols were not only vigilant, they were also numerous.

From the mouth of the Wash to Selsey Bill, a sea-distance of under three hundred miles, there were now nearly 300 armed patrol vessels constantly at sea out of a total of over 700. From Harwich to Plymouth more than 40 destroyers were stationed, of which a large number were at sea every night, resting their crews and refuelling in daytime. Between the Tyne and Plymouth there were, in addition to 6 cruisers, 25 fast minesweepers and 140 minesweeping trawlers. A sufficient force to ensure that the enemy should not come unheralded, those who manned it were determined that he should not come unopposed. After long weeks of waiting it was perhaps their chief anxiety that he might not come at all.

That same night, far away to the north, Admiral Forbes in the *Nelson* led a division of the Home Fleet, comprising the carrier *Furious*, the light cruisers *Naiad* and *Bonaventure* and the 6th Destroyer Flotilla, on a sweep towards the Norwegian coast. His depleted forces had recently been weakened still further by the detachment for *Operation Menace* – the Dakar expedition – of a battleship, 2 cruisers and 4 destroyers, and his strong desire to carry out offensive patrols across the North Sea had been curbed by Admiralty restrictions in force for the duration of the invasion crisis. Nevertheless, enemy supply ships having been sighted off Norway whence, in addition, rumours were coming of an impending raid on Iceland, he decided to despatch the remaining available Home Fleet vessels – *Repulse*, *Berwick*, *Norfolk* and 4 destroyers – to investigate to the north, whilst he himself steamed on to the east. Early on the 7th his aircraft intercepted two enemy vessels and attacked.

Damaged, but not sunk as at first believed, the two supply ships headed back to port; and in a little while Berlin was informed of these renewed enemy activities in the north. Added to the news from Paris of hostile patrols off the French coast, the naval staff began to reassess – slowly, in default of their once speedy interception service – the strength and intentions of the British fleets in home waters.

The reduced day-time patrols on the 7th made few sightings, but from Dover large numbers of craft could be seen off Calais – tugs, trawlers, self-propelled barges – and it became evident that, while there was not the slightest movement across the southern North Sea towards England, ships and small craft in considerable quantities were sliding down the coast to French harbours south of Cap Gris Nez. The invasion force was building up, even if the direction of the intended attack was far from certain.

Late that afternoon large numbers of German bombers passed high over the eastern entrance to the Dover Strait and turned westward up the Thames estuary. Something new was developing; and the crews of waiting vessels wondered whether they would not soon see their bases go up in flames. But when, at dusk, the destroyers and MTBs of the Nore Command again moved out to sea and laid off their several courses towards France, it was from London that a fearsome glow could be seen far to the west, whilst overhead the German bombers rumbled back in their hundreds, not to the naval bases, but to the capital.

Throughout Britain it was a night of activity and tension. The night on which the *Cromwell* code word was issued to the Home Forces, and was taken by many to mean that invasion had already started. Out in the Channel, meanwhile, the patrol vessels kept watch. Four MTBs of Coastal Forces reconnoitred Boulogne, where stress of weather hindered operations, and then went on to Calais where, despite extreme darkness, a number of ships were identified, two hits scored with torpedoes and a tug heavily machine-gunned. Four destroyers from Portsmouth, standing in to the French coast, watched Calais until dawn, when it became disappointingly clear that the enemy had not moved.

During the morning when the ships of the Nore Command fell back upon Sheerness and Harwich they saw, while still far out to sea, a vast pall of smoke overspreading the Thames estuary, reaching out many miles from west to east. But again, as they presently discovered, it was not the naval bases that had been laid in ruins.

Over London during darkness the Luftwaffe had flown nearly 300 bombers. Bomber Command, too, had been active that night; to attack the Channel ports it had sent 37 aircraft. If London still lived, so did the invasion fleet. And whilst Naval Group West mentioned the activities of the British bombers, it also complained of the presence of British patrol vessels.

In the course of Sunday the 8th the weather began to show signs of deterioration, so that with low cloud and freshening westerly winds in the Channel, it appeared improbable that the enemy, despite the favourable tides, would attempt to launch his attack on either that or the following night. However, although the numerous daily patrol flights made by Coastal Command – under Air Ministry control, but in close co-operation with the Admiralty – revealed no forward movement towards the English coast, aircraft of the Photographic Reconnaissance Unit brought evidence of a steady accumulation of shipping in Dutch and Belgian ports, and it was appreciated that any improvement in the weather might be followed by an immediate sailing.

To the responsible British authorities the direction of the impending attack was still a matter of conjecture. The low-lying Essex and Suffolk coasts with their numerous rivers and creeks and sandy beaches, the Kent promontory with its sheltered bays, the proximity of both areas to London, the massing of the invasion fleet in Dutch and Belgian ports, all seemed to indicate an attempt upon either side of the Thames estuary. With this view the Commander-in-Chief Home Forces, General Brooke, agreed; for it was on this day that he noted in his diary: 'Everything pointing to Kent and East Anglia as the two main threatened points.'

Some additional colour was given to this opinion by the investigations, on two successive nights, of naval reconnaissance forces. Admiral Drax at the Nore, pleading with the Admiralty for more cruisers, had stressed on September 4th that 'to hit Germany hard by destroying an invading force we need gunfire and plenty of it'; but given the enemy's naval weakness he already possessed a sufficient gunfire potential to make his presence felt.[1] In co-operation with the Portsmouth Command,[2] and despite worsening weather, he sent out a combined reconnaissance and raiding force on the night of the 8th.

The force, consisting of the *Aurora* and *Galatea* (2nd Cruiser Squadron), 5 MTBs from Harwich, 6 destroyers from the Nore and 5 from Portsmouth, split up into five parties. The first visited Ostend where 2 MTBs entered the harbour, circled among the shipping at speed and fired four torpedoes, all of which hit; two medium-size steamers were sunk, two others exploded, one of them disintegrating. (Air reconnaissance next day showed three new wrecks in the harbour.) At Dunkirk the second party of MTBs went right up the approach channel, but, in poor visibility, found nothing; on their way out they picked up three German airmen from a sunken bomber. At Calais 3 destroyers, ahead of the *Galatea*, nosed their way in as far as the entrance to the inner harbour; it was very dark and they saw nothing; there were no patrol boats, no searchlights,

---

[1] On the 4th he had received into his command the Town-class cruisers *Manchester*, *Southampton* and *Birmingham*, detached from the Home Fleet.
[2] Admiral Sir William James.

no enemy fire; the Germans appeared to be asleep, and the place was therefore left undisturbed for future operations. At Boulogne the *Aurora* and 3 destroyers found visibility extremely bad; no ships were seen, but as their presence was known a sharp bombardment of the inner harbour was carried out. Meanwhile, the 5 Portsmouth destroyers, proceeding at 25 knots, swept down the coast from Le Touquet to the mouth of the Seine. Unfortunately, bad weather interfered with operations; in the words of the War Diary, 'a very violent and sustained thunderstorm broke and the low cloud and heavy rain reduced visibility to a very low compass'.

No further sightings were made and, by morning, all ships of the force had returned to their bases unharmed.

During daylight on the 9th the heavy gun batteries between Gris Nez and Wissant came to more violent life than usual. Opening fire at six in the evening they kept it up until after eleven, by which time nearly two hundred rounds had been thrown at Dover and its immediate vicinity. That little of military importance was achieved is shown by the Dover report: 'Casualties and material damage remarkably light; five persons, including one soldier, were killed, two houses and a garage demolished and about twenty other buildings damaged.' The bombardment – to which the 14-inch gun at St. Margaret's Bay replied – did seem, however, to be yet another presage of forthcoming invasion.

After dark 6 destroyers each from the Nore and Portsmouth and 4 MTBs repeated the previous night's operations, save that the Portsmouth ships reversed direction, sweeping the French coast from St. Valery to Le Touquet. Weather conditions were improving, but visibility was still poor and few sightings were made. Short bombardments were carried out by the Nore destroyers at Calais and Boulogne, but the Portsmouth flotilla had nothing to report. By the Admiralty these meagre results of reconnaissance – which, because of the weather, could not be amplified from the air – were regarded as supporting the views of those who thought that an attack was more likely upon the south-east coast than upon the south.

The fact was, though the Admiralty could not know it, that the groups of shipping frequently observed from Dover to be moving round Gris Nez to the south were being passed to Le Havre and Cherbourg after dark, whilst other transport groups farther to the east had been delayed by the continuing bad weather and rough seas, and there was thus a nightly shipping gap from Dunkirk to Boulogne. A gap purposely maintained by the enemy; because, if the material effect of naval gunfire – and of Bomber Command's larger but still relatively small contribution – was very far from being decisive, the effect upon the minds of Naval Group West was steadily growing. In the area of the narrow seas, they were beginning to perceive, the Royal Navy possessed not only 'gunfire and plenty of it' but also the determination to use its flotillas offensively in the time-honoured manner. Calais and Boulogne lay too close to British bases to provide safe anchorage at night; transports allotted to these ports would not be brought in until the last moment. Almost unintentionally, therefore, they preserved the mystery of the empty ports and so kept for a few days more the much-needed element of operational surprise.

In Berlin, however, the German naval staff preferred to insist upon the part played by the weather in delaying the invasion fleet assembly; and in this sense they summed up the news from Paris in their report on the 10th. 'The weather conditions', they wrote, 'which for the time of year are completely abnormal and unstable, greatly impair transport movements and mine-sweeping activities for *Sealion*.'

The picture of practically all operations at sea being brought to a standstill solely by the weather was not very flattering to those who manned the German ships. The functioning of the enemy's Auxiliary Patrol and Coastal Forces was not halted by the 'completely abnormal' conditions which to British crews, however sorely tried by the long vigil, did not seem to differ very much from the usual ingredients of an English summer. The small ships continued to keep watch in the Dover Strait and the narrow seas; and on the night of the 10th the destroyer divisions went out again to sweep the enemy-held coast. Those from Portsmouth, sweeping from Le Havre to Boulogne, were unlucky. But three ships from Harwich had the good fortune to find a number of trawlers and barges off Ostend; and upon these they opened fire with good effect.

[15]

Ten Nights to Decision: II

WHATEVER THE CONCLUSIONS to be drawn from events at
sea, there could be no doubt that weather conditions had
reduced the fury of the Luftwaffe assault on Britain during the
8th, 9th and 10th, just as they had curtailed Bomber Command's attacks on the invasion ports. This enforced reduction
in intensity did nothing to disturb the sanguine expectations
of the German air staff; it may even have seemed to them an
advantage that, after the deadly hammering of the 7th, the
people of London should be granted a brief respite to let the
truth of their plight sink in; with all the more horror would they
anticipate the resumption of attacks even heavier and fiercer.

As for the British fighter defences, although it had to be
admitted that they had not yet been utterly destroyed, it seemed
crystal clear to Göring that henceforth they could do little to
affect the issue by day and nothing at all by night. In daylight
on the 9th it was far more the cloudy and uncertain weather
than the interference of Fighter Command that diverted some
of the German bombers from their allotted targets; and when,
after a relatively quiet day on the 10th, the attack on London
was driven home by day on the 11th, it was evident that the
resistance was no longer very effective. For once the Luftwaffe
staff rightly estimated that their own aircraft losses had been
markedly less than those of their opponents;[1] and on the
strength of this, and summarising the results of the past fortnight, they reached the conclusion that strategic victory was
now very near. Were the attacks upon England, and especially
upon London, to be continued with the maximum available
strength by day and by night, then air victory might become
total victory in a matter of days. With this view Hitler was in

---

[1] Post-war official losses for this day were: 29 British and 25 German.

full agreement: the air assault must go on, *Sealion* must wait. On the 11th he did not so much postpone the operation as defer the warning-date order for three days.

Here, as Räder saw, was the clear-cut divergence. On the one hand, the pursuance of the policy of 'absolute' air war. And much as he detested Göring he was inclined to agree with a bombing policy which he had supported from the start; now that some thousands of Londoners had felt 'the impact of war' upon their persons it was at least conceivable that further heavy blows might urge them to throw up the sponge. On the other hand: *Sealion*.

After all the intensive preparations, the vast and painstaking shipping organization was nearing completion. With improving weather the last ships of the transport fleet would soon have moved to their assembly points, filling to capacity the ports from the Scheldt to Cherbourg; they could not be held there indefinitely, the damage to the German economy would be far greater than that which even the heaviest British raids might cause in the Channel ports. And the Army was waiting, chafing at the delay; its anti-aircraft guns and amphibious tanks were ready, its supplies piled up on the docksides. Brauchitsch and Halder might shake their heads at the narrowness of the front, they still regarded the British land forces as of poor quality; Rundstedt was still confident of the result once his mobile troops were able to break out of the beach-heads; the Supreme Command staff expected Hitler would order the crossing to be made on the 23rd, the Navy's optimum date.

Sealion must not sail; postponement was essential to avoid a resounding defeat; of that Räder and his staff were now convinced. On July 19th they had told the Supreme Command: 'So far the enemy has not needed to use his fleet fully, as a matter of life and death, but the landing operations on the English coast will find him resolved to throw in fully and decisively all his naval forces.' The truth of that clear-sighted statement had now to be faced: 'It would be irresponsible to do otherwise', Räder had said.

No comfort was to be drawn from past history. Not unless the bombing of London brought surrender could political intrigue or wavering be counted upon to bring about a weakening of British naval strength in the south-east such as had opened the Thames and the Medway to de Ruyter. None of the hesitation that had cost England Minorca and Byng his life was likely to be displayed in the Channel. The clumsy handling and irresolution that had caused Graves to fall back before de Grasse off the Chesapeake Capes was not to be expected upon the flanks of *Sealion* off the coast of England. Intelligence reports and the news from Paris had made that much clear, and a good deal else besides.

Visual observations from the French coast, from the decks of minesweepers attacked in the Dover Strait, from belated air reconnaisance of the harbours of southern and eastern England, had combined to banish any remaining hope of a faulty disposition of British naval forces. Along the lines of concentration from those bases at which they had been identified large numbers of destroyers, several cruisers and at least two battleships[1] could reach the *Sealion* crossing area within a few hours of the alarm being given. And to ensure that this alarm should be given in good time the small vessels of the Auxiliary Patrol held the sea in all weathers, whilst every night the fast MTBs and the destroyers swept down the invasion coast with impunity.

There could be no doubt about it: the eight-pronged first wave of the invasion fleet could not take its departure wholly unperceived. Nor, once perceived, could it make the crossing and landing without disastrous loss – *unless* the outflanking British warships were attacked in their bases, violently, persistently and forthwith. No such attack could be made from the sea and, since it was now known that an attack from the air was neither contemplated by Göring nor expressly ordered by the Führer, the conclusion was obvious. *Sealion* must not be allowed to sail. To this end Räder worked, biding his time.

Naval Group West gave him the evidence he needed. A closer scrutiny of operational realities than was available to the distant

---

[1] At Plymouth, as well as the *Revenge*, was stationed the old target battleship *Centurion*, rigged to appear fully operational.

focus of Berlin or to the remote and airy perspective of the
Bergdorf had revealed to the sinking faith of the staff in Paris
all the holes in the naval plan. The enemy's alertness and
strength, their own fatal weakness; the constant enemy patrols,
his minesweeping and renewed minelaying; their own limited
sweeping and laying baulked by the enemy's watchfulness when
not by the weather; the dislocation caused by almost nightly
raids from the sea as from the air; these things combined to
bring about a state of anxiety bordering on defeatism.

Hitherto their reports had been brief and factual, dealing
with the equipment of ports from the North Sea to the Bay of
Biscay and with minor operations in the Channel. Now they
stressed the shortcomings: the delays, the accidents, the shortage
of minesweepers and of mines. Increasing enemy activity was
noted, casualties emphasized, the effect of gunfire from the
Dover batteries exaggerated.

'Interruptions,' it was noted in Berlin, 'caused by the enemy's
air force, long-range artillery and light naval forces have for the
first time assumed major significance. The harbours at Ostend,
Dunkirk, Calais and Boulogne cannot be used as night anchorages for shipping because of the danger of English bombing and
shelling.'

Anxious to excuse themselves in advance for any disturbance
to the time-table, Naval Group West reported that 'owing to
these difficulties, further delays are expected in the assembly of
the invasion fleet'. But for this fear there were few grounds.
With improving weather, the entire assembly would be completed, Berlin knew, within three days. What then and subsequently would befall was in Hitler's hands.

On the same day as that on which they received the disturbing reports from Paris, the 12th, the German naval staff set
down their considered opinion of the forthcoming operation.

'The air war is being conducted as an "absolute air war",
without regard to the present requirements of the naval war,
and outside the framework of *Operation Sealion*. In its present
form the air war cannot assist preparations for *Sealion*, which
are predominantly in the hands of the Navy. In particular one
cannot discern any effort on the part of the Luftwaffe to engage

the units of the British Fleet, which are now able to operate almost unmolested in the Channel and this' – they added rather unnecessarily – 'will prove extremely dangerous to transportation. Thus the main safeguard against British naval forces would have to be the minefields which, as repeatedly explained to the Supreme Command, cannot be regarded as reliable protection for shipping. . . .'

The 'main safeguard' – not the heavy guns, nor the U-boats, not even *Herbstreise*; only the unreliable minefields. All very well to explain to the Supreme Command; it would have been wiser to get these obstinate facts through to Hitler. He it was who had insisted in July upon the mine-barriers as an essential prerequisite to invasion; yet now, with the mine-barriers still unlaid, he was preoccupied with the air war, concerning which the naval staff could but enter their blunt though logical verdict in the War Diary.

'The fact remains that up to now the intensified air war has not contributed towards the landing operation; hence, for operational and military reasons the execution of the landing cannot yet be considered.'

The Army Command and the Luftwaffe Generals might indulge their easy imaginings; to the trained naval mind the unvarnished truth was conclusive. With a British fleet in being, the invasion 'cannot be considered'. But would Hitler perceive the truth in time? At his command *Sealion* had been created, the invasion fleet assembled – at what cost to Germany! On the 14th his orders, and his alone, would decide its fate. The fate, it might be, of the Nazi *Reich*. Räder braced himself for the encounter.

On the 13th further events came to strengthen his argument. That night, in improving weather, the English bombers were out again over Belgium and Holland, concentrating their attack upon Ostend where barges and lighters were sunk or damaged and supplies destroyed upon the quaysides, causing confusion and disorganization. The 'hindrance' was still a long way from being 'decisive', but it was at least noteworthy that the enemy force employed was stronger than on previous occasions; the Royal Air Force was still far from the desired annihilation.

Of far greater significance for the ultimate fate of the *Sealion* fleet was the continued 'unmolested' manoeuvring in the nights of the 11th and 12th of the enemy's light naval forces in the Channel. From the Nore, Portsmouth and Plymouth the destroyer divisions, the MTBs and fast motor gun-boats came forth to sweep the enemy-held coasts from Holland to the Channel Islands. Behind them the cruisers waited at instant readiness, but there was no call for their services; no opposition, other than some inaccurate shelling by shore batteries, was encountered and the British ships proceeded almost leisurely on their way, reconnoitred the ports and sought their targets. The mouth of the Maas, Flushing at the mouth of the Scheldt, Ostend, Dunkirk, Calais, Boulogne, Le Touquet, Cherbourg – all were entered, examined or shelled, while the smaller craft attacked minesweepers and trawlers, saw them slide sinking into the darkness. When they had done, the ships steamed back to England unharmed.

To observers on the spot, reporting back to the headquarters of Naval Group West, the chances of a successful *Sealion* crossing in ten days' time may now have appeared rather less than negligible. What hope was there? Reliance upon the mine-barriers, supposing them to have been laid in time, was vain. The great guns at Gris Nez might bark ferociously, their bite was ineffectual. No faith could be placed in the U-boats. The invasion fleet itself was, for all practical purposes against destroyers and cruisers, entirely defenceless. The Luftwaffe could do nothing by night, and Richthofen, commanding the dive-bombers now concentrated behind Calais, had expressed grave doubts of the ability of his force to do anything by day. What was left? *Herbstreise?*

On the 11th, Churchill had broadcast from London; his summary of the invasion possibilities had been impressive. Amongst other points he had mentioned that 'there are some preparations made of ships to carry an invading force from the Norwegian harbours'.

To the German naval staff it looked as if the cat had been let out of the bag rather too soon; the more so when, on the

13th, Admiral Forbes brought the *Nelson* and *Rodney*, with the cruisers *Naiad* and *Bonaventure* and 8 destroyers, from Scapa to Rosyth where the *Hood*, fresh from a refit, was already waiting. Not even the 'Light Cruiser Squadron' would be safe on its Autumn Journey at S-Day minus 1.

Two considerations made necessary the division of the Home Fleet at this time. On the one hand, it was essential to maintain at Scapa a force capable of moving swiftly against a break-out attempt in the direction of Iceland; and this force consisted of the *Repulse*, the carrier *Furious*, the cruisers *Norfolk*, *Berwick* and *Glasgow*, the anti-aircraft cruiser *Coventry*, and 4 destroyers, to which were presently added the new cruisers *Kenya* and *Nigeria* (each twelve 6-inch guns). On the other hand, the move of a strong force to Rosyth, prompted by the apparent imminence of invasion, was made imperative by the information passed to Admiral Forbes by the Admiralty on the 13th, suggesting that a large-scale German invasion in the south-east would be supported by 'every capital ship they can make available'. And, the signal added, such ships were still thought to include the *Bismarck*, *Scharnhorst*, *Gneisenau*, a pocket battleship, and probably the two venerable battleships, as well as several cruisers.

With this force at Rosyth ready to support the forces in the southern North Sea, the anti-invasion dispositions of the Royal Navy were brought, by the 14th, to their maximum strength.

[16]

Ten Nights to Decision: III

READING BETWEEN THE lines of the transactions at the Commanders-in-Chief conference called by Hitler in the afternoon of September 14th, some significant facts emerge. Something also of the changed outlook, not of the principal actor but of some at least of the other participants. They were uneasy. Events had carried them far from the comfortable assurance of mid-July when the Führer had opined that the war was already won, but that England had not yet recognized the obvious. Britain's military situation did not now seem quite so 'hopeless' as had been affirmed in Directive 16. The war had still to be won that autumn. But how?

Before the conference began, Räder, no doubt anxious lest Hitler should have summoned this unusual three-services meeting for the express purpose of ordering *Sealion* to proceed, handed in a short memorandum in which he summed up the arguments against the seaborne invasion and underlined the importance of the air attacks 'particularly on London', which 'must continue without interruption' and 'be intensified without regard to *Sealion*'.

Possibly to show that he was already well acquainted with such opinions, Hitler then opened the proceedings with a surprise announcement. According to Räder's notes: 'The Führer has come to the conclusion that it would, after all, be wrong to call off *Operation Sealion* altogether as he had apparently planned to do on September 13th.'

This was news indeed; a complete turn-about and the first anyone had heard of the intention to 'call it off altogether'. But perhaps the reasons were not very far to seek.

Obsessed though he was with the mirage of total victory, Hitler cannot have been ignorant of the *Sealion* situation and its dangerous implications. His capacity for absorbing information was considerable, and he was aware of the unfavourable position at sea. But although he could see that it would be a mistake to challenge England's naval power directly, he still believed that, in the matter of the seaborne invasion, air power could replace sea power. The air onslaught upon Britain was what mattered most. That and the weather.

'The air attacks have been very effective,' Räder quoted him as saying, 'and would have been more so if the weather had been good.' Although he failed to mention that the same weather applied to the enemy, he was not overstating the case.

The spectre of British sea power had never brooded more heavily over the conference table; deliberately, one must suppose, Hitler made no mention of it. 'The degree of air supremacy necessary to justify executing *Operation Sealion* has not yet been reached', he explained. 'For this reason *Operation Sealion* is not yet practicable.' Nothing about naval affairs; but the omission mattered little to Räder. At hearing that the Führer now agreed with what the naval staff had so strongly argued he could only rejoice. He would rather that Hitler had followed his impulse to call off the operation altogether; but against this wise course he had to listen to a rather involved dissertation.

'If the pressure of the imminent landing were added to further air attacks, the total effect would be very strong after all. For not one attack is decisive, but the total effect produced. If *Operation Sealion* were called off now, British morale would be lifted and our air attacks would be easier to bear.'

Just then it was Räder's morale that was lifted, at the prospect of postponement, so that he was emboldened to play again the card he had first laid upon the table on July 11th. He had, he said now, 'always been of the opinion that *Operation Sealion* should be the last resort and that the risk is very great'. He stopped short of mentioning the purely *naval* risk; the subject being a painful one he followed the line of least resistance. The 'absolute air war' was foremost in Hitler's mind. Räder gave it support in the terms of his memorandum.

'In the event of good weather' – the weather again – 'the Luftwaffe must first be given the opportunity to intensify the attacks, especially on London, regardless of *Operation Sealion*. These attacks may decide the outcome of the war.'

Of two gambles he had chosen the least desperate. The naval staff had stated unequivocally that 'in its present form the air war cannot assist preparations for *Sealion*'. There was no hope of getting Hitler to order an abandonment of the absolute air war in favour of an all-out attack upon the British fleet, nor would there be time for such an attack to be effective before the next proposed warning date, the 17th. *Sealion*, therefore, must take second place.

'*Operation Sealion*,' he went on, 'must not be abandoned now, however, for the reasons given by the Führer.' But, he argued skilfully, since the situation 'as regards the safety of *Operation Sealion*' could scarcely be expected to change in the course of the three days gained by the postponement suggested by Hitler, he proposed a longer postponement 'until October 8th or 24th' -- the next most favourable moon-tide conjunction.

The Führer would have none of this. Despite his expectation of victory through air bombing, he was loth to give up the idea of seaborne invasion, of the pressure of German troops on the soil of Britain as the final symbol of conquest. He alone, he declared, would decide on September 17th 'whether the operation is to take place on September 27th or not'.

Nevertheless, something had been gained and Räder may well have sighed his relief, buoyed by the secret hope that with nothing being done in the meantime to help *Sealion* a further postponement on the 17th would become inevitable. All the more galling must it have been to hear a sudden and wholly unexpected intervention from Brauchitsch.

'The Commander-in-Chief, Army, declares that the Army no longer attaches such great importance to a landing at dawn, so that the time element involved can be reconsidered.'

So! The Army was still keen to make the crossing despite the naval staff's warnings, still confident of its chances in England despite the lack of total air mastery. For the sake of invasion it was ready to cross in daylight -- under cover of smokescreens! What of the British fleet? Had the Army forgotten that as early as July 19th the naval staff had stated in plain language: 'It cannot be assumed that the Luftwaffe alone will succeed in keeping the enemy naval forces clear of our shipping. . . .' An opinion that had never been contradicted by any competent authority, nor, in particular, by the commander of the dive-bombers. What would the Army do – Räder might wonder – when, during the crossing, by day or by night, the 'sea front' became active?

Räder allowed himself to be faintly sarcastic. 'As far as the Commander-in-Chief, Navy, can find out, this sudden change in the Army's initial stubborn demand can be traced to the fact that the front-line Generals, like the Navy, are opposed to a night crossing.' At least they had learned that much; had digested the naval staff's warning of the inextricable confusion likely to occur in the darkness of the Channel. But, in dismissing the idea, Räder may have thought that with any luck postponement would have been made permanent long before the new daylight plan could be worked out in detail.

Räder turned away from Brauchitsch and his smokescreens to give further support to the air war. 'In discussing the air attacks on London, the Commander-in-Chief, Navy, supports the view of the Chief of the General Staff, Air' – Jeschonnek, Göring was not present – 'namely, that the attacks on targets of military importance will not suffice to produce mass psychosis and large-scale evacuation, since the residential areas are some distance from the docks. . . .'

Hitler interrupted him. He wished, Räder noted, 'to reserve deliberate attacks on residential areas as a final means of pressure and as a reprisal for British attacks of this nature'. An ugly piece of sophistry, for Hitler knew well enough what his bombers had already done to London homes.

Räder, after some further argument in favour of the devastation of London, did obtain one small concession in favour of *Sealion* from the air staff. 'As soon,' Jeschonnek told him, 'as the positions of the heavy British coastal batteries have been established, they are to be attacked by dive-bombers of the Luftwaffe.' Not even for this task could reliance be placed upon the long-range guns at Calais.

That night the Supreme Command's directive was issued

over Keitel's signature. It ordered the continuation of air attacks against London, with terror attacks 'not to be employed at present'. But, although *Sealion* was 'postponed', a new order was announced for the 17th and meanwhile 'all preparations are to be continued'.

It was not as much as the naval staff had hoped for. Räder's decision to plump for the absolute air war and get *Sealion* postponed, if not finally at least until October, had not paid the expected dividend. With the Army still very much in the market for a land battle and the Luftwaffe making its all-out bid for strategic victory, pressure might yet be brought to bear upon the Führer, the sense of whose final decision was far from certain. 'Not one attack is decisive, but the total effect produced.' To Hitler the addition of invasion to the total effect might prove irresistibly attractive.

For *Sealion* was now ready. By the 15th all essential transports, motor vessels, trawlers, self-propelled barges, tugs, launches and lighters were lying moored in their appointed harbours. Supplies had been assembled; the first-wave divisions had completed their training and were ready to embark; the previous postponement had given time for the entire organization to be brought up to almost instant notice. None of this could be hidden from the Führer; he had but to nod his head and *Sealion* would put to sea.

With the return of better weather the Royal Air Force bombers were increasing the scale of their attacks on the invasion ports, once more disproving some of the Luftwaffe's larger claims to command of the air. But, however disturbing the attacks, the number of aircraft available to the British and the weight of bombs they could drop on any given night were still quite insufficient to inflict a decisive blow. So far, less than 10% of the assembled shipping, including lighters, had been sunk or damaged; given available replacements, it was safe to predict that there would be by the 26th (the new sailing date) an ample margin of transport.

A fact already adumbrated had, however, now emerged from the indecisive results of these enemy air attacks, although it was one that added nothing to *Sealion's* prospects in the long run. In the naval staff's memorandum of July 19th it had been laid down that 'the gaining of air supremacy is vital to the possibility of assembling the requisite naval forces and shipping in the relatively restricted area of embarkation'. The point had been stressed time and again since then, both by the naval staff and by Räder himself in conference with Hitler who had recognized its validity. Even their enemies across the Channel believed that the assembly of an invasion fleet would not be feasible so long as a British bomber force existed.[1]

And yet it had been done. During July and August there had been few targets for the enemy's Air Force to strike at in the invasion ports; now that the ships were there he had not the strength to extirpate them. If, from the air, he could not destroy the concentrated fleet lying stationary in harbour, he could not hope to destroy it under way when, from Ostend to Le Havre, it would be spread out over more than a hundred miles of sea. Even if daylight were chosen for the operation, a considerable part of the crossing must still, given the fleet's low speed, be made at night when neither British nor German air forces would be able to intervene effectively; and, even supposing that at this late hour arrangements could be made to meet the Army's suggested afternoon-tide landing, what could the enemy do from the air by day? He had neither dive-bombers nor torpedo-carriers in any useful quantity; the unlikely intervention of his small force of night-bombers would be more costly than effective; his fighters, even thrown in at sea-level, could not sink the barges nor stop the transports. What the German dive-bombers, highly specialized, efficient and numerous, had not been able to achieve against the Channel convoys was not likely to be accomplished by the Royal Air Force against *Sealion*.

But this last argument applied also to the Luftwaffe: it had not conquered the convoys, nor closed the Dover Strait to British warships. Although by day and close into the Franco-Belgian coast it could protect the assembling transports, it

---

[1] Churchill, *The Second World War*, Vol. II, page 281: 'The preparation of the embarkation ports, the assembly of the transports ... were impossible without protection from British air attack.'

could not, as had been clearly stated by Räder and by the naval staff – and was presently to be admitted by other German authorities – expect to hold off the numerous British warships now certain to close in upon either flank during the crossing.[1] And if those warships became mixed up with the smoke-screened *Sealion* vessels in a short range mid-Channel mêlée, neither air force would be able to lend an effective hand for fear of hitting its own ships.

The deduction was self-evident. For the invasion of Britain, at this stage of this war, air superiority was not decisive. It could not replace superiority at sea. The only safeguard for *Sealion*, by day or by night, was a naval force capable of holding and defeating the enemy's assembled warships. This naval force Germany did not possess. Worse than 'a desperate gamble', as Räder called it, the project could not be deemed a serious operation of naval warfare.

The anxious days of waiting passed slowly for the naval staff. Little came in from Paris, but that little was not good. After a night's respite due to stormy weather the Portsmouth and Nore destroyers were off the French coast again from the 14th to 16th, whilst the untiring auxiliary patrols in the Channel kept watch without cease. Nelson's dictum that 'our first defence is close to the enemy's ports' was being all too well observed. And behind the naval patrols the English coastal defences were being strengthened. On the 15th one of the 14-inch naval guns in St. Margaret's Bay opened fire and ranged over the downs behind Gris Nez. Though its importance was over-estimated, it, and the other heavy guns identified in the Dover area, boded ill for the flank of *Sealion* that, entering Sandgate Bay, was to move to the capture of the first and vitally necessary port at Folkestone.

For the supporters of *Sealion's* postponement rather more encouraging news came from the air reports. Whilst at night British bombers were at work again over the invasion ports, by

---

[1] This point being vital to the case for the decisive influence of British naval power in frustrating *Sealion*, the testimony supporting it has been summarized in Appendix B.

day the Luftwaffe over England was not having it all its own way. On the 14th the end had seemed to be near; during attacks on London the fighter opposition had been ineffectual, the respective losses light and about evenly matched. But next day, although some 220 bombers distributed a heavy load of explosives over the capital, the British fighters were more numerous and more active; losses were relatively heavy and in a ratio of two to one in favour of the enemy. Clearly, the 'absolute air war' battle was not yet ended and the naval staff, with a poor weather forecast to aid them, drove the point home along the old lines of argument.

'The enemy air force is still by no means defeated', they noted in the War Diary. 'On the contrary it shows increasing activity.' And: 'The weather situation as a whole does not permit us to expect a period of calm.'

To their relief Hitler followed the same line. On the 17th, with news of half a gale blowing in the Channel, he decided to postpone *Sealion* 'indefinitely'.

Only ten days previously Räder had assured him that: 'The execution of *Sealion* appears possible if attended by favourable circumstances regarding air supremacy, weather, etcetera.' In what way were the circumstances so unfavourable as to make the operation impossible now? That the weather was momentarily bad did not necessarily indicate bad weather on the proposed S-Day. Total air mastery over England had not been won, but it was not essential over the Channel for the purposes of *Sealion*, since air power alone could neither sink nor safeguard the barges. What remained? The one factor that counted above all else: the inescapable 'etcetera' – the implacable *'undsoweiter'* of British naval might. Many things contributed. It alone was decisive.

[17]

Into October

RÄDER WAS NOT out of the wood yet. 'Indefinitely' did not mean 'for good'. In fact to the naval staff it meant only that now there was not even a provisional date; the Führer might order a new S-Day at any moment with no more warning than the agreed ten days, if that. In some ways the uncertainty made matters worse than before the postponement.

For this Räder himself was partly responsible. At the Führer conference on the 14th he had said: 'If we wish to avoid loss of prestige, it will be permissible to abandon *Operation Sealion* only at the moment of maximum air successes, on the grounds that it is no longer necessary.'

But that 'moment of maximum air successes' would be the moment when England collapsed, when *Sealion* might be launched with diminished danger from naval interference to topple the crumbling defences by producing the Führer's 'total effect' of several simultaneous attacks. And collapse was what Hitler, on the basis of Göring's estimates, still expected almost from day to day.

'We have a good chance to force England to her knees', Halder quoted him as saying on the 14th. 'Even though victory in the air should not be achieved before another ten or twelve days, Britain may yet be seized by mass hysteria.' Twelve days would bring him to the 26th or, stretching patience a little, to the end of the month. Given the now recognized dangers of an opposed crossing, the 'mass hysteria' must come first; so that in all probability *Sealion* would be ordered to set out during the second week of October, and the entire organization must therefore be maintained at full strength and ready to move at short notice. One slight but significant change was made; on the 19th Hitler agreed to the release of ten *Herbstreise* steamers, and of a further six from the invasion fleet, to Norway where the occupation forces were seriously short of shipping. 'At the same time,' a new Directive commanded, 'it should be arranged so that in good weather 8–10 days (from the issue of the warning order) remains sufficient for reassembling the ships in the embarkation harbours at the appointed time.'

To the naval staff this situation was unsatisfactory in the extreme. Räder had warned Hitler, on the 14th, that 'should *Operation Sealion* fail . . . the enormous effect of the air successes would be minimized.' But the 'enormous effect', whose intensification he had himself advised, might at any time be magnified by the boastful Göring, upon whom Hitler still placed undue reliance, into a renewed claim of approaching total victory. Brauchitsch with his smokescreens – 'making the Army', Halder claimed, 'independent of the dates set by the Navy' – might apply pressure through the Supreme Command. Together, Army and Luftwaffe optimism might swing Hitler to the sudden ordering of a new but still premature S-Day.

The situation was dangerously vague; all too tempting to one of Hitler's quicksilver moods and uncertain temper, concerned as he was with the necessity of bringing England down before the autumn storms and fogs closed in upon the Channel coast. To clarify the position, to make postponement definite – after the Supreme Command Directive on the 19th had made it still more indefinite – the naval staff summed up in the War Diary the obvious facts concerning the 'sea front'. For once no mention was made either of the weather or of the unessential air supremacy. A clear and concise statement, it dealt solely with naval matters.

'1. The preparations for a landing on the Channel coast are extensively known to the enemy, who is taking more counter-measures. Symptoms are, for example, operational use of his aircraft for attacks and reconnaissance over the German operational harbours; frequent appearance of destroyers off the south coast of England, in the Dover Strait, and on the Franco-Belgian coast; stationing of his patrol vessels off the north coast of France; Churchill's last speech, etc.

'2. The main units of the Home Fleet are being held in

readiness to repel the landing, though the majority of
the units are still in western bases.

'3. Already a large number of destroyers (30) has been
located by air reconnaissance in the southern and south-
eastern harbours.

'4. All available information indicates that the enemy's
naval forces are solely occupied with this theatre of
operations.'

It was not the whole picture. The naval staff had not yet
discovered the full extent of the Admiralty's dispositions; and
the reports from Admiral Canaris's Foreign Intelligence Department were feeble and at times nonsensical. But it was at least
factual, and the Royal Navy continued to give it point.

To the regular feature of nightly destroyer sweeps along the
invasion coast, other measures were added as new or recon-
ditioned ships joined the anti-invasion fleet. In the night of
September 29th the 15-inch-gun monitor *Erebus*, fresh from a
lengthy refit, crossed the Channel and bombarded Calais. Here,
at last, was a target worthy of the great batteries of heavy guns
behind Gris Nez. The monitor's designed maximum speed was
12 knots, but she could now make only 8 and, in the choppy
waters of the narrow seas, she was almost unmanageable. The
great coastal guns opened fire. They failed to hit her.

There was nothing spectacular about the steady pressure of
naval patrols and flotillas. No blazing fire-ships bore down upon
the *Sealion* transports as upon the Armada at Gravelines; no
costly inshore assaults, such as Nelson had attempted at Boulogne, were made in the roadsteads. Night after night, often in
ominous silence, the flotillas from Portsmouth and the Nore, the
MTBs from Dover and Harwich made their presence felt. By
the world at large little was heard of their activities; they did
not go unnoticed by the German naval staff.

From Plymouth[1] in the night of October 11th the battleship
Revenge, with 7 destroyers and 6 motor gun-boats, closed in and
bombarded Cherbourg. . . . It was too much. In the Channel,
destroyers, MTBs and uncounted patrol vessels; upon either

[1] Western Approaches Command. Admiral Sir Martin Dunbar-Nasmith, V.C.

flank, 15-inch guns; in England, no '*mass hysteria*'. Next day Hitler called off the invasion plan. It was one of the major decisions of the war.

'From now until the spring,' the Supreme Command announced in the Führer's name, 'preparations for *Sealion* will be continued solely for the purpose of maintaining political and military pressure on England.'

Inside Germany the shipping problem had become acute. Her whole economy, and that of occupied Europe, depended -- as Räder had stressed more than once – to a very large extent upon inland water transport. The withdrawal of, in all, nearly 2,000 barges and lighters and almost all the tugs had brought this vital traffic virtually to a stop; so that together with the serious shortage of coastal and Baltic shipping caused by the requisitioning of 170 steam transports, and the additional calling in of 20,000 seamen, even the most ardent *Sealion* enthusiast could see that an already grave situation might easily become disastrous were the invasion fleet to be maintained in idleness much longer. The roads and railways, overburdened in any event, were wholly inadequate to shoulder the vast additional load normally carried upon the great rivers and the canal network of Western Europe. Were Germany to become involved in war with Russia as the Führer intended she should be, with the *Sealion* fleet still in being she would start the campaign half-crippled.

The losses from air bombardment and naval shelling had also to be taken into account. Up to September 21st, 21 transports and 214 barges and lighters had been sunk or damaged, amounting to $12\frac{1}{2}\%$ of the total,[1] and the figures had been augmented since then. But, although few replacements were available, these reductions did not by themselves endanger *Sealion's* prospects; they had been allowed for by the naval staff in their calculations of shipping required. Such losses were, in fact, acceptable if, with *Sealion* launched, the invasion were successful, just as the

[1] This total, however, did not include the large assembly of motor-vessels, trawlers, launches, etc. (notably at Le Havre where losses had been negligible). Elsewhere, the loss of tugs was put at only 1·4%, and the *overall* loss at this time was therefore probably below 10%.

Luftwaffe's losses in daylight over southern England were acceptable if the absolute air war ended in Britain's collapse and surrender. They were not acceptable if the invasion fleet were to be retained 'solely for the purpose of maintaining political and military. pressure'. That way madness lay; Germany would defeat herself.

Under pressure from the naval staff, the Supreme Command bowed to the obvious, Hitler tacitly consenting. Towards the end of October the great fleet that should have borne a conquering army to England began to disperse. The transports steamed away by night to safer harbours and more profitable employment in the Baltic; the trawlers and drifters went back to the fishing grounds; the tugs and self-propelled barges towed their strings of lighters up the deserted canals and rivers. The life-blood began to flow again through the arteries of Nazi-dominated Europe.

The damage caused to Germany by the invasion assembly could not be made entirely good. For three months the top priority given to the naval staff for the requisitioning and adaptation of suitable vessels, which had seriously diminished both essential commerce and war-time industry, had held up the building of U-boats; and time lost by the disruption could never be wholly regained. That Hitler, knowing their effect, had sanctioned and indeed insisted upon these measures, is perhaps the surest sign of his determination to invade and conquer.

Nor did all those vessels which had assembled in September return in October. Air bombardment together with naval shelling and torpedoing had sunk or seriously damaged nearly 100,000 tons of various shipping. On the German side it was almost the only tangible result of the great invasion plan. Almost, but not quite; for against it must be set the greatly increased sinkings in the Atlantic, due to the temporary withdrawal of British escort vessels, which gave the German Navy much encouragement for the future.

For the Army it was manifestly absurd to keep troops in training on the beaches or practising embarkation in the ports when there was no longer any fleet for them to sail in. The Supreme Command directive of October 12th had stated that 'should the invasion be reconsidered in the spring or early summer of 1941, orders for a renewal of operational readiness will be issued later. In the meantime military conditions for a later invasion are to be improved'. They could hardly be improved by retaining arms and equipment upon the bombed quaysides; nor, with orders for a 'renewal of operational readiness' not to be expected for six months, was there much point in keeping a large number of earmarked divisions concentrated in north-eastern France and Belgium. Some resumed their less strenuous duties as garrison troops in the French Occupied Zone; some were withdrawn, and presently moved to the east. Tension was relaxed, the summer's excitement died down; in a little while men began to forget.

Although it still had an official existence, the *Sealion* plan was shelved. In its heyday it had possessed a force of considerable strength, a Grand Army of 500,000 men. With its amphibious tanks and mountain guns, its anti-aircraft and rocket batteries, its heavy guns at Gris Nez and its Luftwaffe 'artillery', its 20,000 bicycles and 50,000 horses, its carefully calculated scale of reinforcement and its invasion fleet of over 4,000 vessels, it had been equipped, under experienced and resolute commanders, with almost every item necessary to ensure success. Only the essential element had been lacking: Command of the sea.

The moral effect of the abandonment of the invasion plan upon either the German Army or the cowed civilian populations of western Europe is hard to estimate, but it was not negligible.

Certainly the truth could not be kept hidden for very long. The troops who had been training upon the beaches or practising embarkation in the ports were not in any doubt when the autumn weather broke and heavy seas came pounding along the bleak Channel coast, when training ceased and the transports moved away from the harbours and roadsteads. An appearance of readiness might be kept up in the coastal areas, the men knew well enough that no invasion would be attempted that winter. They might feel relieved; they were aware that something had gone wrong.

As for the people of the Low Countries and north-eastern France, they no longer depended entirely upon gossip, the evidence was before their eyes; the barges were moving up-stream again, away from the coast whence came more frequently now a distant mutter of guns. And if German aircraft in their hundreds still roared up from the airfields, other aircraft some-times droned high overhead and far inland, aircraft at which the Germans fired furiously; the war in the air was continuing. The war at sea too – the very claims of unending success made by the German news service proved it. The old rumour of easy conquest had long since been falsified; Britain was still in the fight. In the wintry darkness there appeared the first glimmer of hope.

Presently there were other items of news – the Nazis could not suppress them entirely – of British naval actions in the Mediterranean, off Genoa, at Taranto; of Italian defeats in North Africa and Greece. As yet these things, if they heartened the French, could scarcely impair the disciplined quality of the German troops; but those troops were a little less exuberant. They had begun to perceive that, after all, the war might be a long one and just occasionally they voiced their doubts of its outcome.

'We drove into France,' said a German officer that autumn, 'at sixty kilometres an hour. One day we may have to drive out of it at eighty.'

But such doubts were seldom more than intuitive. To the immense majority the strength of Germany's position seemed unassailable, even though final victory had been unexpectedly delayed. Unaware of the causes as of the gravity of the failure to subdue Britain, few had any but the faintest premonition of what might yet be forced upon the mighty *Reich* by the steady pressure of sea power.

[18]

Twofold Victory

HITLER, LIKE OTHER tyrants, was incapable of honest and enduring gratitude to any man. He showed none to Räder. Conveniently forgetting the Grand-Admiral's truly remarkable achievement in creating and bringing forward a vast invasion fleet within the space of six weeks, he remembered against him his advice to postpone *Sealion*; so that when, early in 1943, he accepted his resignation – forced by Göring's intrigues and personal spite – he accorded him none of the customary honours and rewards to which long and outstanding service entitled him.

And yet it was Räder who, in days when victory seemed sure, had saved him from resounding defeat. For there can be no question that, had *Sealion* sailed, it would have been reported and attacked either at the moment of departure or on passage, or else fatally mauled upon the beaches and during the despatch of reinforcements. Nothing then available to the Germans on land, upon or under the sea or in the air could have prevented the irruption into the crossing area of the Channel of hundreds of armed vessels, of in all some 60 destroyers and of at least 8 cruisers backed on either flank by heavy ships all at immediate notice.

In his memorandum on methods of dealing with an invasion attempt in 1801, Nelson wrote that, once the invading vessels had touched the shore, 'the bows of our Flotilla will be opposed to their unarmed sterns' and that thereafter 'the courage of Britons will never, I believe, allow one' – of the enemy – 'to leave the beach'. In 1940 the picture of a neatly aligned row of sterns waiting for the toe of the naval boot may have seemed as unrealistic as the suggestion that the 'courage of Britons' would alone have been sufficient to annihilate the invaders had they succeeded in landing; yet it cannot reasonably be denied that, given a resolute land defence capable of pinning down the disembarking Germans for at least a few hours, the hastening destroyers and cruisers from Portsmouth and the Nore would have made short work of the stranded lighters and of the transports moored in open roadsteads, and that they could have done this work without the assistance or protection of the Royal Air Force, the Luftwaffe notwithstanding. Thus it might well have come to pass that not one of the landed enemy would have been 'allowed to leave the beach' without permission of the defenders.

That the tenuous line of supply and reinforcement would subsequently have been cut is beyond peradventure. Once *Sealion* was launched, and small initial beach-heads presumably established, it could not be countermanded; the second échelon, and no doubt the second wave, had to proceed if the first échelon was not to perish. The slow-moving transports, the barge-clusters wandering upon the tidal streams would have been intercepted by day or by night, at their point of departure, on passage or upon arrival. The small ships of the Auxiliary Patrol were too vigilant to be surprised, too numerous to be eluded once the alarm had been given; the destroyers within brief steaming distance were too fast as well as too numerous to be diverted from their objective by German dive-bombers, even discounting the help of Fighter Command. With the cruisers in support, there was 'gunfire and plenty of it' – anti-aircraft fire, too – and those ready to apply it lacked nothing in skill and resolution. *Sealion* could not get through. Despite the advent of air power the prospects for invasion were much the same as when St. Vincent declared: 'I do not say they cannot come. I say they cannot come by sea.' For the immediate conquest of Britain there was still no other way.

In the assault upon the invasion fleet the probability of British naval loss had to be accepted, whether caused by the few small enemy warships, by mine or torpedo, by dive-bomber or even by the guns at Gris Nez. But, however serious any further weakening of the fleet, especially in destroyers, the losses would be more than outweighed by the advantage gained in halting *Sealion*. Even were the enemy, after an initial landing, to press on with his ten-day reinforcement plan, naval losses normally regarded as crippling would be acceptable if they resulted in the destruction of perhaps a hundred thousand German troops and all their equipment. In August 1805, referring to the perils besetting Calder's force, Nelson said that 'by the time the enemy had beat our fleet soundly, they would do us no harm this year'. The sinking of half the destroyers in the Southern Commands, had it been accompanied by the defeat in action of *Sealion*, would have kept Hitler quiet for a very long time.

What matters is that this was how the enemy saw it. To Räder and his Admirals it was a case for simple logic.

Initially the Army had demanded, with Hitler's full approval, the transporting in a single armada of a large, mechanized and heavily gunned force and its deployment upon a wide front. The naval staff was unable to undertake the transport of the required force because, owing to British naval action, they could not find enough shipping; and they could not guarantee the safety of the wide front because, again owing to British naval action, they had not the necessary warships.

Subsequently, as the German naval staff saw more and more clearly, the Royal Navy's dispositions and the unrelenting pressure of its flotillas off the invasion ports reduced the chances of a safe crossing, with even a small force on a narrow front, virtually to zero. The only possibility of success lay in the destruction of the greater part of the British fleet. The German Navy had not the power necessary to effect this destruction; the Luftwaffe did not attempt it, did not even plan it. The seaborne invasion had to be ruled out before disaster ensued.

The facts seemed plain enough. But the facing of displeasing facts and the following of an argument to a logical and unpleasant conclusion were not Hitler's strong points; had they been so, he would scarcely have gone to war in the first place. As for the Army – Brauchitsch, Halder, the staff of the High Command – in matters concerning land warfare they could be logical enough, but their logic, with their responsibilities, ended where the sea began. To them the wording of the Führer's directives, based upon their own conceptions of strategy, was satisfactory and sufficient. 'A landing in England is possible . . .

this operation is dictated by the necessity of eliminating Great Britain . . . units of the Navy will do the work of engineers.' Then let the Navy get on with the job. It was as simple as that.

Hitler might listen attentively to Räder's objections, it was the Army's – and Göring's – views that he chiefly heeded. He might signify 'the Führer agrees' at the naval conference table, his subsequent orders were frequently at variance with the agreement. With Räder's plea, on July 11th, that invasion should be used 'only as a last resort' and his forthright declaration: 'I cannot . . . advocate an invasion of Britain', he was in apparent accord; five days later, after consulting with the Army, he issued the *Sealion* directive. On July 19th the naval staff's forceful explanation of the dangers facing the seaborne invasion reached the Supreme Command; yet when, on the 21st, Hitler lectured his Staff, although he described the 'exceptional daring' needed to cross a sea 'dominated by the enemy', he mentioned as essential prerequisites only 'complete mastery of the air, the operational use of powerful artillery in the Dover Strait, and protection by minefields'. The certainty, upon which the naval staff had dwelt, that the enemy would 'throw in fully and decisively all his naval forces' was almost wholly discounted in this and subsequent discussions. Hitler was not merely, as he had once told Räder, 'a coward at sea'; he was also incompetent as a naval strategist. Having lost the Trafalgar campaign he thought to win the Trafalgar battle without ships wherewith to engage the enemy.

His incompetence – for his under-estimation of the effect of British naval power upon *Sealion* amounted to that – is displayed in Directives 16 and 17. In the first he said only that it was 'desirable' to 'pin down' the British fleets, but at least he suggested that this should be achieved by means of sea and air attacks. In Directive 17, however, he negatived even this vague desirability by ordering that 'air attacks on enemy warships and merchantmen may be diminished, unless particularly advantageous targets offer themselves;' and the Luftwaffe was told to direct its attacks 'primarily against the aircraft themselves, their ground installations and supply organizations, also against the aircraft industry, including plants producing anti-aircraft material', after which it was to turn to 'the ports, especially against establishments connected with food supply, and also against similar establishments in the interior of the country'. But although 'particularly advantageous targets' continued to offer themselves daily off Sheerness and Harwich, neither Hitler nor Göring took any further notice of them. A final paragraph to Directive 17 boldly declared: 'The Navy is authorized to begin the projected intensified naval warfare . . .' How this was to be done without either warships or naval aircraft was not explained.

Against this incompetence as against military optimism born of ignorance of maritime affairs, and a measure of ineradicable military prejudice against the junior service, Räder fought with tact and tenacity. His position was not a strong one; he had to face a concensus of Army opinion that had become by mid-July entirely favourable to seaborne invasion – and was still by no means unfavourable at mid-September – the opinion of victorious Generals who, of the vaunted influence of British sea power, saw only that it had not prevented them from over-running Poland and Norway, the Low Countries and France, from driving the English out of the continent of Europe and from breaking the blockade. He had to beware of the hostility and personal hatred of Göring, standing higher in the Führer's favour and ever ready to put in a bad word for the Grand-Admiral behind his back; and he had to face across the conference table a man who, from being affable and almost friendly, might at any moment become the tyrant of uncertain temper.

Nor was Räder's character strong enough to resist the will of a ruthless and unprincipled leader. At heart a kindly man, reserved, diffident, he was generally liked by his equals, though by his juniors, from whom he exacted a harshly rigorous discipline, his manner was thought dictatorial to the point of arrogance – but was perhaps only traditionally Prussian. He himself obeyed orders, not blindly but certainly without question. He was a man who *needed* a master. In earlier days he had looked up to the Kaiser as to a stern yet benevolent being not far removed from God; now he regarded Hitler with something of the devotion of a gentle hound to whom the least reproach brings unspeakable pain, the least approval a preview of heaven. Like many another in the Nazi Reich, at times he was mortally afraid of disfavour. Some personal enmity or political intrigue, some professional mistake leading to a sudden decline in the Führer's regard, and degradation might swiftly follow. The thought of Himmler and the Gestapo turned his stomach; he carried, concealed, a pistol for the ultimate defence of self-destruction. He was sixty-four at the time of *Sealion* and not in the best of health.

His doglike devotion to his master, which in the matter of Norway was to bring him into conflict with the customs and usages of civilized nations, was matched by a more admirable loyalty to what he believed to be the interests of his country. Those interests were, he knew, endangered by the invasion plan. Great wars between equally determined opponents are commonly won by the side committing the least number of major blunders; and as a blunder he was aware that *Sealion* would be fatal. Obeying his orders to the letter – he could scarcely have done otherwise without personal risk – he worked patiently and steadfastly against the final error. It took both skill and courage; for a commander who successfully resists being forced into battle by a ruthless military dictator is both a better strategist and a braver man than one who meekly obeys knowing that the outcome will almost certainly be irretrievable disaster. Due credit must be accorded him. Nothing in the end could spare his country from the fate to which Hitler had condemned it; in its hour of victory he could at least save it from rushing down the gadarene slope into a sea of defeat.

He played his cards well. Not a subtle man – lack of subtlety had marred his career between the wars – he had sufficient wisdom to know that one who raised nothing but objections would not sit for long at the Führer's conference table. His attitude was far from entirely negative; he followed the directives, achieved substantial progress, made constructive suggestions, and bowed only to Hitler's final decisions. Although he would certainly have done better to have stressed more frequently the paramount necessity of paralysing the British fleet, he found it more tactful never to miss an opportunity of calling attention to the Luftwaffe, excusing its failures and occasionally praising its progress towards the goal of air mastery. No doubt he did this partly to avert blame from his own service should the Luftwaffe fail, but since he more than half believed in the efficacy of the absolute air war he also hoped to placate Hitler, perhaps even Göring, by his approval and thus, minimising the importance of seaborne invasion, to get *Sealion* postponed until air power had won the day. In this he succeeded; for it was far more the apparent nearness of total victory in the air war than any real understanding of *Sealion's* naval difficulties that caused Hitler to change his mind about the necessity for invasion. But he came perilously near to failure when, on September 6th, he told Hitler that the success of *Sealion* if launched on the appointed date 'appears possible'.

For the next ten days it was touch and go. Räder knew it and feared it; on the 14th, even when a further three days' grace had been granted, he felt bound to rub in once more his 'last resort' view of the operation, coupled with a broad hint of the likelihood of failure and consequent dire results. Not until after the 17th, however, did he at last feel strong enough to allow the naval staff to come out into the open with the reasons, based exclusively on naval realities, that reduced *Sealion* to the level of an empty dream.

II: THE ROYAL NAVY

Räder's victory over the powerful influences favouring the seaborne invasion must not be allowed to obscure the far greater victory won by British sea power over Germany.

For victory there was. One that was gained by the traditional development of an offensive strategy and not merely, as has too often been suggested, by measures of passive and hesitating defence. The foundations of the victory were built up during the first ten months of hostilities in accordance with a time-honoured, aggressive policy which if it did not, in 1939, regard invasion as a very probable danger always had to include the remote possibility as among the perils against which the Royal Navy was bound to guard. Thus, in fulfilling its traditional functions without specific reference to a military thrust at the heart of the Empire, the Navy was incidentally always gaining strength to meet the situation which arose in the summer of 1940.

The invasion crisis falls into two distinct phases: that which became abruptly evident when the Germany Army reached the Channel coast on May 21st and which seemed to grow more menacing with every hour that passed from Dunkirk to the fall of France and after; and the second which began to develop in mid-July and reached its climax in mid-September. The first, by far the most disconcerting, proved in the end to be entirely imaginary; yet at the time, shocked by unparalleled military defeat, impressed by the enemy's deep-laid schemes and lightning approach to their shores, the Government and people of Britain found it quite impossible to believe that, in the matter of invasion, Hitler had prepared nothing at all. The phase had, however, an excellent effect; it aroused the whole population, it brought a million men to the Home Guard, it stimulated production in the armament factories; under Churchill's tireless and versatile prodding it compelled the hitherto somewhat complacent Chiefs of Staff to think again and to act quickly. By the time the first phase had merged into the second Britain's defences, if not everywhere strong, were at least tidy. At sea, against Germany, they had been unassailable from the outset.

The second phase began when Hitler signed the *Sealion* directive. From that moment, unknown to London though the plan was, the accumulated achievements of British sea power relentlessly exerted their decisive influence. (See above: 'The Light-Cruiser Squadron' and 'The Limiting Factor'.)

In 1908 the Committee of Imperial Defence had studied the problem and concluded that the Army in Britain must be of sufficient strength to 'compel an enemy who contemplated invasion to come with so substantial a force as would make it impossible for him to evade our fleets'. And this principle was restated in the Prime Minister's Minute of August 5th, 1940. It was not disproved, but events brought some notable modifications.

In June 1940 the British Army was hardly in a state to

'compel' anything; and although by September it had been so re-equipped and reorganized that, with 16 divisions (three of them armoured) ready to act on the south-coast front, it might perhaps have been able to deal effectively with the 9 divisions of the enemy's First Wave had he been able to land them, to General Brooke the margin of safety appeared dangerously narrow. The British forces could not, in any case, then *compel* the sending of a larger number of German divisions, since the enemy lacked the ships in which to send them. Nevertheless the invasion forces were, once concentrated in the Channel ports, 'so substantial' that 'to evade our fleets' must be an impossibility were the 'fleets' to be present in sufficient numbers. With the Royal Air Force incapable of destroying the invasion forces either in port or on passage, and with the Army far from sure of its ability to defeat the invader once landed, only a strong naval force could with certainty avert the peril first by intercepting and then by denying reinforcement. To this end the Admiralty, accepting for a limited period and a specific purpose the recognized dangers both of air attack and of a weakening of the Home Fleet, brought its cruisers and destroyers to southern bases to maintain, in conjunction with the several hundred smaller craft, constant offensive action off the invasion ports. The enemy, aware of the presence as of the strength of naval forces which he could neither oppose nor dissipate, tacitly conceded failure and abandoned his grandiose plan.

From mid-August on, as the Luftwaffe moved towards the absolute air war, the sensational events of the air battle tended to obscure understanding of those naval developments which were to determine the fate of *Sealion*. Incidents of the daily air combats, in which the losses of each side were almost invariably – and sometimes grossly – exaggerated by the other, so dominated the minds of men, even in high places, that it seemed to many as though nothing, no other force, no other combatants, remained to oppose an invasion other than 'the few' of Fighter Command. The impression was gained that Britain's chances of survival depended so nearly upon success in the air battle that the good results of a single day's fighting could affect the military situation decisively; to such an extent that after mid-September it was put about in some quarters that the possibility of invasion had been ruled out by virtue of an air victory, on the 15th, in which the enemy's losses had inadvertently been over-estimated by nearly 350%.

Belief in the total supremacy of air power was almost universal at the time, and in Britain – after the disasters on the Continent – it governed the views of many in authority. From May to August it was reinforced. On May 15th Air Chief Marshal Dowding, warning of danger ahead were further fighter units to be despatched to the Continent, had made a deep impression upon a meeting of the Cabinet. On the following day his opinions, held with the utmost sincerity, were summed up in the concluding paragraph of a letter to the Air Ministry: 'if the Home Defence Force[1] is drained away in desperate attempts to remedy the situation in France, defeat in France will involve the final, complete and irremediable defeat of this country'. The drain to France had ceased to flow long before the commencement of the battle over Britain, but the main proposition still seemed to be held; namely, that only Fighter Command could defend the nation from a defeat 'final, complete and irremediable'. When the three Chiefs of Staff, reporting to the Cabinet, had expressed their view that 'the crux of the matter' was victory in the air, and when, on August 20th, Churchill had added to this his memorable – and apparently exclusive – tribute to the pilots of fighter aircraft, it began to appear that as a factor for the defence of Britain against invasion the Royal Navy was thought to have lost all practical value.

Räder knew better. Following Hitler's lead, he might believe that Göring's absolute air war would bring about a collapse principally through the devastation of London; in the matter of *Sealion* he and the naval staff had made it abundantly clear that alone command of the sea was decisive. Later knowledge only strengthens the validity of his view.

It was, after all, Germany who held the initiative in 1940, Germany who wished to invade; once the veil of war-fog and propaganda had been lifted, it was Germany and Germany's

[1] i.e. Fighter Command.

naval archives which were best able to supply the reasons why
the invasion had not been carried out. One of Räder's own staff,
Admiral Kurt Assmann, who was actively engaged in planning
the operation and who, both then and much later, had access
to all the documents connected with *Sealion*, was able after the
war to study the affair from both sides and to sum it up carefully and impartially.

This was his verdict:[1]

'From among the prerequisites mentioned as necessary for
carrying out the operation one condition was lacking, a condition which was never discussed and which, given the relative
German and British naval strengths, could not be discussed; yet
one which, even undiscussed, was discernible between the lines
of all our deliberations. It was the *one* prerequisite – whose lack,
early in the previous century, had brought Napoleon's invasion
plans to nought and which, in 1940, could again not be supplied
– *command of the sea!*

'It had been thought possible to replace this lack of command
of the sea with command of the air, or in other words to sup-
plant the enemy's sea power by our own air power. That was
not possible for this operation. In fact, even had good luck
favoured the landing, with acceptable losses, of a fairly compact
invasion army, the main difficulty – the continued supply and
reinforcement of the landed troops in face of an enemy growing
in strength from day to day in his own country – would then
have only begun. It was not to be expected of an enemy over-
whelmingly strong at sea, resolute and prepared for any
sacrifice, that he would in the long run be prevented merely
by mine-barriers and by the Luftwaffe, whose operations were
in large measure dependent upon the weather, from breaking
in with his naval forces and disorganizing the supply line.'

His next paragraph is revealing.

'When the time came for the final decision to be taken, none
of the responsible personalities was ready, despite his knowledge
of the weighty matters at stake, to take a firm stand *against* the
operation. All, however, were inwardly relieved to be able to

---

[1] From *Deutsche Schicksalsjahre*, published by Eberhard Brockhaus, Wiesbaden.
The translation given here is by the present author.

find, in the lack of air mastery, a sound argument which would openly justify them in abandoning the operation.'

By way of postscript to the invasion story Admiral Assmann relates an incident at Führer Headquarters in 1943. In the course of table-talk, Hitler in reminiscent mood 'expressed the liveliest regret at having allowed Räder to talk him out of *Sealion*'. To his regret, clearly demonstrating his continued ignorance of sea power, may be opposed the conclusion reached by the British official naval historian, Captain Roskill.

'The lessons of 1940 appear to reinforce our knowledge that, although continental enemies have repeatedly tried to find a way to invade these islands without first defeating our maritime forces, no such short cut exists.'

To that undeniable proposition but little attention was paid in Britain, then or later. For the resolutely silent service, it remained a silent victory indeed.

Epilogue: 'Lest we forget – '

A SOLITARY AIRCRAFT of ancient design drones across the London sky, heading west. There is a moment's silence; then, with a crescendo rush, the fighters of a new era flash by, and are gone.

September 15th: Battle of Britain fly-past. A reminder of dark days and a fitting tribute to those young men who fought through them so gallantly. But to the great majority of London's millions who, with heads suddenly upturned to the thunder, watch the brief display of air power, the occasion symbolizes the legend of a handful of British fighter pilots utterly routing the Luftwaffe and alone sparing the nation the horrors of invasion and conquest. The Royal Navy is in total eclipse.

That, in 1940, the succession of aerial combats over Britain should have been regarded in all sincerity as 'one of the most decisive battles of all time' was not only an inevitable but also an invaluable assessment. It focused attention and stimulated, by underlining a heroic resistance, the combative spirit of the nation and its determination to fight on whatever the odds. From London, as from the south-eastern counties, the combats could frequently be seen; spectacular fighting high in the summer sky marked by tracer and condensation trails, by the smoke of burning aircraft thought always to be German; and it was because the combats were visible, whilst all other action against the enemy remained invisible, that upon the skill and courage of 'the few' there were concentrated the anxious hopes of all Britain and half the world. The very fact that the Luftwaffe, which seemed with apparent ease to have subjugated Europe, was being met and fought gave the battle an added significance, enhanced by reports of huge German losses, and greatly served the cause of Britain in America.

The commencement of the day and night bombing assault at the end of the first week in September, if it did little to diminish the country's confidence, did even less to encourage the view that a decisive air victory was close at hand – unless, the wags remarked, it turned out to be the enemy who was winning. Nor did the total of supposed enemy losses on the 15th, although it was the largest announced so far, appear to mark the day as one of memorable achievement. It was not until later, when the enemy had turned from costly daylight raids to the seemingly endless routine of night attacks, when summer had become autumn and autumn winter, that the period of hard-fought day-time combats over England came to be classed officially, not as a first danger painfully averted, not as a breathing-space narrowly gained, but as an overwhelming and all-decisive victory comparable with Trafalgar. In some quarters Dowding was likened to Nelson; and from then on until the ending of the war the magnitude of the summer success, with its officially sponsored and never corrected figures of enemy aircraft losses, remained one of the central themes of British propaganda at home and abroad.

All this was natural enough at the time. It may even have been essential, in the grim autumn of 1940, to chalk up at least one notable gain where all else seemed loss and to give the British people something upon which to chew to alleviate the pain of protracted bombing. At a time when, although the vast majority of the people were quietly resolved to carry on till final victory was theirs, the means whereby that victory should be won were almost beyond conjecture, the announcement that a decisive success had been scored against the Luftwaffe, if not very convincing to the bombed-out inhabitants of towns and cities, provided at least a glimmer of light in the reigning darkness. The hasty miscalculation of 185 enemy aircraft destroyed on Sunday, September 15th, at the height of the assault on London, came as a godsend.[1] And although the figure was soon known in responsible quarters to be false, no correction was issued while the war lasted. Even then the figure might have been allowed to stand, together with some other only slightly less fantastic inaccuracies, had the secret documents captured in Germany not been shared with the Americans. The rectification was forced.

After the war, however, when the true figures of German aircraft losses in the battle over Britain became known – and

---

[1] The correct figure for that day was 56 enemy aircraft destroyed.

their publication caused considerable chagrin – and when the German plans for *Sealion* were officially released, it appears strange, almost disquieting, that no complete reappraisal should have been made of the role played by the respective services in the invasion situation of 1940. Here history – and it is the British histories of British action that will be read by future generations – seems to have been distorted by a war-time view necessarily restricted by the requirements of prestige, propaganda and military security. For the most part the war chroniclers, diarists and historical writers have one after the other, and often using almost identical phraseology, continued to uphold and expound the official and popular line that it was in the main, if not wholly, the Royal Air Force which caused the abandonment of *Sealion* and that therefore the *air battle alone* 'determined the whole course of the war'.[1] Each relates in detail the day-to-day fluctuations of that battle, describes the combats, gives the losses suffered or inflicted, mentions bombs dropped and civilians killed. Each dwells upon relative air strengths and monthly aircraft production, analyses the composition of the enemy air fleet, makes clear the enemy intentions and how, it would seem, they were almost invariably frustrated by the Royal Air Force, as much by technical superiority as by brilliant leadership on the ground. Each devotes space to the German plans for invasion, to the German Navy's hopes and to their complaints against the Luftwaffe for not subduing British air power. Scarcely one takes sea power into account or says anything of the Royal Navy, unless compelled to do so by the context of some passage quoted from the enemy. It is as if an account of the battle of Waterloo were made to end with the repulse of the French cavalry charges.

Some there are who go so far as to insinuate that the Navy, fearing air attack, was less active than it might have been. Only the official naval historian speaks out in favour of the senior service.[2] But even then, whilst a general account of the Admiralty's measures to meet invasion is given, the details of naval operations in the Channel and off the invasion ports are

[1] Basil Collier, *Leader of the Few*.
[2] Captain Roskill, *The War at Sea*, Vol. I.

mostly omitted. The reason for this appears to be the statement by the Editor of the 'History of the Second World War' Series, Professor J. R. M. Butler, to the effect that because of something the Prime Minister (Attlee) said in 1946, 'the historians have thus felt themselves under no obligation to tell the story of operations in the same detail as was thought appropriate in the case of the war of 1914–18'. If the naval historian is not to give details of naval operations, one may perhaps ask: Who will? The question is the more pertinent since other volumes in the series give the fullest details of *air* operations, to the greater obscuring of the Navy's work.

Whatever the reasons, this over-emphasis of the value of air power in 1940 has worked to the detriment of a clear understanding of the value of sea power; so that it will be useful to determine, after the lapse of many years, precisely what the Royal Air Force did and did not do.

To take the negatives first, as they appear to result from the evidence so far examined:

1. *Fighter Command* could not, by itself, make it impossible for the enemy to invade by sea in September 1940.

2. *Bomber Command*, able to find targets on the invasion coast only after September 1st, had not the strength to inflict decisive damage upon the invasion fleet before S-Day (September 21st–26th). Nor could it destroy the fleet on passage.

3. *Coastal Command*, co-operating with the Navy, might have given warning of the departure and passage of the invasion fleet in conjunction with the naval patrols; it could not by itself prevent either the crossing or the landing.

4. *Fighter Command*, despite the heavy losses it inflicted upon the Luftwaffe, was unable to prevent a very considerable amount of daylight bombing from mid-August to past S-Day. (In the course of 24 days in September 1,200 tons of bombs were dropped in daylight attacks on Lon-

don alone. The amount might well have been greater but for patches of bad weather.)

5. *Fighter Command* and the anti-aircraft defences generally were quite unable to prevent the heavy night bombing which, beginning in August, continued throughout the autumn with scarcely a break and no appreciable loss to the Luftwaffe. (In the course of 24 nights in September 5,300 tons of bombs were dropped on London alone.)

Before making a further examination of points 4 and 5 above, the positive results gained by the Royal Air Force must be stated.

Hitler, in Directive 17, ordered Göring and the Luftwaffe to 'overcome the British Air Force', including its airfields and ground organization, 'in the shortest possible time'. This task they failed to perform, near though they came to success. They were prevented from performing it by the efficient organization and technical superiority of Fighter Command and by the stark heroism of its pilots.

Therein lies the true victory. For the first time the great German Air Force had met with a determined opposition which it was unable to crush. For the first time after the swift and apparently easy triumphs of Poland, Norway, the Low Countries and France it was made clear that Hitler was not going to have it all his own way with Britain; and throughout the world the effect was immense. For the first time a mighty German plan had gone agley, a Göbbels-proclaimed time-table had been upset. Hitler had not lost the war, not yet; he had not even been decisively defeated, for worse was to follow; but he *had* lost, in a preliminary engagement, the prestige of invincibility in the air.

Unfortunately, if unavoidably, the measure of the British success was made, both then and later, almost wholly dependent upon the numbers of aircraft lost on either side. At the time both sides exaggerated their claims, the Royal Air Force through wishful thinking coupled to careless checking, the Luftwaffe because of a lying propaganda service and its own

arrogant belief that the enemy was certain to be defeated whenever encountered. For as long as the war lasted the British
claim stood at something over three enemy aircraft destroyed
for every one lost to the Royal Air Force. When exact figures
became available after the war the claim was reduced until it
stood at two to one. But even this is not accurate.

The figures officially given show that between July 10th and
September 6th the Royal Air Force lost 550 *fighters* and the
Luftwaffe 956 aircraft *of all types*. This is not two to one, and
if account is taken of British aircraft *other than fighters* lost through
enemy action in the air or on the ground the ratio is still further
lowered; so that it would probably be fair to say that during
this phase the British lost rather more than 600 aircraft 'of all
types' and the Germans rather less than 1,000. The comparative
scale of losses is therefore barely five to three. Given that the
Royal Air Force could afford its actual losses in fighter aircraft
even less than the Luftwaffe its losses in aircraft of all types,
the margin of victory was so narrow that, had it not been for
the failure to 'overcome the British Air Force' *within the expected
time-limit*, the Luftwaffe might well have been able to justify
earlier its claim that total victory was near. It was that justifica-
tion, bringing forward the decision to launch *Sealion*, which
Räder and his Admirals so greatly feared.

But victories are not necessarily dependent upon the number
of men killed, of ships sunk or of aircraft destroyed. Of the truth
of this there are plentiful examples in history; but perhaps the
closest analogy in the matter of air operations prior to 1940 is
provided by the First World War. For four years on the Western
Front the Royal Flying Corps, and later the Royal Air Force,
consistently maintained a policy of despatching over enemy
occupied territory ever-growing numbers of aircraft of all types
and for all purposes, covered by strong fighter forces. The great
majority of these aircraft flew by day and, since the enemy's
air defence was both stubborn and skilful and his aircraft
frequently superior in performance and armament to those of
the attackers, the grand total of losses suffered by the British
was many times greater than that inflicted upon the Germans.
The policy was, however, officially justified on the grounds that

it was in the right spirit and necessary to the conduct of military operations; and, at the time of the Armistice, it was generally believed to have contributed to winning the war. When, in 1940, the Luftwaffe tried much the same policy, although the destruction of large numbers of German aircraft was for Britain an encouraging sign it seems scarcely logical that the defenders' victory should have been measured by those numbers alone.

Nor was the victory of Fighter Command complete, as will have been seen from points 4 and 5 above. The Luftwaffe was not, after all, stopped dead. It was not, after a single decisive encounter, dismissed like a tattered armada, never again to issue from its continental bases. Of its initial repulse the great value lay in what it promised for the future. At the end of the first round the supposedly weak challenger, condemned by his 'hopeless' military situation, was still on his feet and full of fight; the invincible conqueror had been sent back to his corner with a bloody nose and some of his teeth missing; something had been gained and the free world rejoiced.

But the end was not yet certain. The daylight attacks continued long after the memorable 15th; were interrupted by stormy periods, to be resumed whenever the weather was favourable and kept up well into October. On October 16th General Brooke, fearing the weakness of his defences in the 'Ramsgate salient, the bay south of it, Deal, etc.', noted in his diary that the 'most recent reports point to preparations for an invasion-try' with a 'force being assembled in the Scheldt'; on the 17th he noted that 'evidence is amassing of an impending invasion . . . Rotterdam filling up with shipping'; and on the 24th he commented that, although the weather was unsuitable, it was 'unwise to assume all safe' that night because the moon and tide were 'most favourable'. That by this time *Sealion* had been postponed till the spring matters little; the fact was not known in Britain. What does matter is that General Brooke was apparently very far from accepting the theory that Fighter Command's relative success in the daylight air battles had made invasion impossible.

To Admiral Forbes it might well seem that the authoritative view of the importance of victory in the air offered a valid argument for the return of Home Fleet ships: the 'crux of the matter' (according to the Chiefs of Staff) was to be found in the air battle; in that battle (according to the official figures) the enemy had been 'soundly beaten'; *ergo*, the invasion threat had been dissipated and the anti-invasion ships could be released. To the Admirals in the southern Commands searching the French coast, as to General Brooke anxiously watching the Kentish promontory, the threat still seemed real enough.

In the upshot Admiral Forbes was right, inasmuch as the invasion had already been cancelled. It was not because of German aircraft losses, or because the Luftwaffe had conceded victory to the Royal Air Force, that *Sealion* was abandoned; but because, as Forbes had always maintained, Britain's command of the sea was still unchallenged. Without command of the sea the invasion fleet could not safely proceed, whether or not air superiority had been gained or lost. Räder knew it; Hitler, whatever his subsequent regrets, was compelled to submit to it.

The opening sentence of Chapter XVI (page 281) in Volume II of Churchill's *Second World War* reads: 'Our fate now depended upon victory in the air.'' The accuracy of this statement, although several authoritative writers have repeated the sentence and those which follow it in terms so nearly identical as to suggest a common source, is not supported by naval evidence either British or German.

Moreover, the next sentence but one, already quoted in part, sets forth: 'The preparation of the embarkation ports, the assembly of the transports, the mine-sweeping of the passages, and the laying of the new minefields were impossible without protection from British air attack.' Not only is the qualification 'impossible' entirely inapplicable to the performance of the tasks named, but Churchill himself has already contradicted it ten pages earlier. At the foot of page 271 (Volume II, *The Second World War*) he states: 'Yet, despite delays and damage, the German Navy completed the first part of its task.' It would be fairer to say the first *two* parts; the preparation of the ports and the assembly of the transports had both been accomplished. The other two, mine-sweeping and laying would be attempted

at night, free from air interference. Churchill continues: 'The
10% margin for accidents and losses it had provided was fully
expended. What survived however did not fall short of the
minimum it had planned to have for the first stage.' A grudging
admission, it none the less partly invalidates the further statement on page 281 that 'the result' – of both preparations and
crossing – 'therefore turned upon the destruction of the Royal
Air Force and the system of airfields between London and the
sea.' The German Navy had brought the invasion preparations
to completion without the achievement of that 'destruction'
which, by itself, could do little to reduce the risks of the crossing.

Another view held by Churchill, and developed by other
competent writers, concerns the Luftwaffe's switch, on September 7th, from its persistent attacks on Fighter Command's airfields and ground organization to the mass assault on London.
Of Göring's action in ordering this switch, Churchill says no
more than that 'by departing from the classical principles of
war . . . he made a foolish mistake'; but since others have
magnified this into a 'major error' and even a 'decisive' turning-
point of the war the switch and its alternative merit a careful
scrutiny.

Had Göring maintained his heavy attacks upon Fighter Command, what would have been the probable result? Air Marshal
Park (Commanding 11 Group, responsible for the air defence
of south-east England) wrote at the time that 'had the enemy
continued his heavy attacks against Biggin Hill and the adjacent
sectors and knocked out their operations rooms or telephone
communications, the fighter defences of London would have
been in a perilous state during the last critical phase. . . .'[1] This
is a long way from saying that only Fighter Command stood
between a practically defenceless country and invasion – and
Park never did say so – but since that suggestion has been
strongly advanced in other quarters it may briefly be examined
here.

Supposing the Luftwaffe to have continued their attacks upon
the vital sector stations it would have taken them, allowing for

[1] Quoted by Basil Collier in *The Defence of the United Kingdom, 1939–45* (Official
War History Series).

the fluctuations of the weather and the daily fortune of war, at least a week so to reduce the organization of Fighter Command that it could no longer put up a strong and efficiently co-ordinated defence in the south-east. This would have brought the date to the 14th, the day of Hitler's postponement confer-ence, when the German air staff, although it could hardly have exceeded the optimism of the reports it had already made, would doubtless have claimed the 'local air mastery' which it had been ordered to gain in Directive 17. It seems, however, in the highest degree unlikely that because of such a report Hitler would thereupon, that same day, have given the *Sealion* warning order. Räder would certainly have stuck to his 'last resort' plea as also to his warning of the consequences of failure, doubtless pointing out that not *all* the enemy's air forces had been destroyed – the bombers would still have been coming over the invasion ports at night – that there were still fighters and fighter airfields north of the Thames and west of Portsmouth, and, above all, that the British fleets were still in being. Hitler, it can scarcely be doubted, would have confirmed the postponement to the 17th, albeit with brighter hopes for the future.

There would then have been two possible alternatives to the assault on London. Either Göring could continue the pursuit of absolute air mastery and move progressively northward over England, destroying airfields, factories and other military objec-tives as he went. Against a stubborn if diminishing resistance, and allowing for the bad weather which in fact eventuated, he could not have taken much less than ten days to accomplish the task, even supposing Fighter Command in the south-east – but not elsewhere – to have been wholly ineffective. This would have brought him to the 27th, the last advisable S-Day, at which time it is safe to say that Britain, whatever the damage to her economy and inner defences, would still not have sur-rendered; and the fleet would still have been intact and ready to intervene upon the *Sealion* flanks. Given the necessity for the ten-day warning period, a further postponement, to October, would have been just as imperative as it came to be in fact.

Or, the alternative, Hitler might have ordered the Luftwaffe – after its presumed local subjugation of Fighter Command by the 14th – to throw everything, as from the 15th, into a concentrated assault upon the anti-invasion flotillas and their essential bases at the Humber, Harwich, Sheerness, Portsmouth and Plymouth. Here again the crux of the matter, if *Sealion* were to be launched that year, was time. The weather ruled out operations on the 16th and 17th and, though improving, remained poor until after the 21st; for the first five or six days the attacks would, at the most, have been scattered and ineffectual. Thereafter only five days would have remained before S-Day on the 27th, and in that time the hope that the whole of the British naval forces within range, together with their essential port facilities, could be so reduced as to ensure an unopposed passage for *Sealion* and its subsequent reinforcements was much worse than forlorn. Ships and their bases were not without anti-aircraft weapons; the ships could be moved, smaller ports and harbours made available during an emergency. Even if withdrawn to more remote bases whence the distance would be too great for an interception of *Sealion* on passage, the ships – reinforced from the Home Fleet, by small ships from less threatened areas, by the last remaining escorts from the Atlantic – would still arrive in time to cut the invasion supply line.

The immediately decisive air assault upon the fleet was not practicable; the Royal Navy could not be destroyed in a week, nor yet in a month. Räder and the naval staff would have liked to see something of the sort attempted; the proposition did not commend itself either to Göring or to Hitler; it was not even considered. The 'pinning down' of the British fleet 'shortly before the crossing', ordered in Directive 16, remained 'desirable'; nothing was done to make it effective. From the thoroughly vague commands contained in Directive 17 no naval plan was developed.

Britain had to be brought down before the winter; that was the immediate aim and purpose of German strategy at mid-September. And, as Hitler saw it, there was one sure way in which to achieve it despite British command of the sea: the absolute air war, concentrated on the capital and carried out by day and by night until the nation gave in. By retarding the *Sealion* order for three days and by advancing the date of the air assault's commencement, ten days could be allowed for the London attack to take effect. Göring and the air staff were certain that collapse would follow within the time limit; Räder was more than half convinced. Occupation, unopposed, could follow on the 27th.

Seen in this light the 'switch' to London of the German bomber force on September 7th does not appear to have been quite such a 'foolish mistake' as Churchill suggests. Although doomed to failure for reasons which are given below, it was a calculated plan. Without it *Sealion* could not sail at all; if it succeeded *Sealion* would not be necessary, save to convey an occupation force. 'We have a good chance of forcing England to her knees', Hitler had told Halder at the climax.

German success in the absolute air war depended upon the fulfilment of two conditions. First, the bomb-load in explosives and incendiaries must be sufficient so to damage or destroy all essential services, centres of communications, power installations, administrative buildings, banks, docks, factories, warehouses and the like that all normal activity should be brought to a standstill and any remaining military resistance rendered nugatory. But, although neither of the principal combatants appreciated the truth at the time – so powerful upon men's minds had been the earlier results of Luftwaffe bombing – the aircraft at Göring's disposal could not deliver a bomb tonnage great enough to paralyse a country as developed industrially as Britain, with its vast ramifications of road, rail and sea transport, its well-organized and smooth-running local services, fire brigades, hospitals, police and the rest. In theory the more than 700 bombers concentrated in northern France and the Low Countries could deliver, on an average over a period of weeks, something like 500 tons of high explosives every twenty-four hours; in fact, for the month of September, the average was no more than half that. It was not enough. Whether distributed over the 800 square miles of the London area, spread over the industrial midlands or aimed at the principal ports, the load dropped was insufficient, given the type of bomb then in use and the limited power of the explosives available, to gain the desired total paralysis of the nation. It could, and did, cause serious damage; it could not inflict mortal injury. Nor could it be delivered fast enough; long after all hope of *Sealion* in 1940 had been abandoned, Göring and the Luftwaffe were still striving after their unattainable goal.

Everything, then, depended upon the fulfilment of the second condition. This was that the inhabitants of Britain's towns and cities, of London especially, should be demoralized and cowed into submission by bombing attacks continued, day after day and night after night, until the mounting horror and devastation had proved too much for human minds. For Hitler to order that 'terror attacks' should not be 'employed at present' was but begging the question; terror was the essential concomitant of a policy designed to induce in the population such a state of 'mass hysteria' as would set a term to any further resistance and, through panic, despairing flight, chaos or open revolt, compel whatever government remained in power to offer surrender. In this phase of the 'battle', given a ratio between day and night attack of approximately five to one in favour of the night when the air defences of Britain were for a while practically non-existent, the Luftwaffe was in fact waging war against the minds and bodies of the British people and scarcely at all against the fighting services, and it was therefore upon the steadfast character of the population as a whole, and of London in particular, that the issue in large measure depended.

Much has been made by the war chroniclers of the element of British victory discernible in the gradual change by the Luftwaffe from day to night attacks. It is argued that the change was compelled by the heavy losses inflicted during the daylight battles of August; that it, together with Göring's 'major error' on September 7th, was the salvation of Fighter Command and thus, by implication, of England; and that it led to a sensible diminution of Luftwaffe bombing effectiveness, since German aircraft were unsuitable and their crews untrained for night operations. Against this must be set the German air staff's opinion that although their losses had been disappointingly heavy, during unexpectedly protracted fighting, they were acceptable in view of the apparent nearness of decisive success, but that, in the absence of any defence during the hours of darkness, it was only logical to prefer the inexpensive night to the costly day. As for decreased efficiency during the hours of darkness, ever since the fall of France the bomber crews had been gaining experience in numerous small-scale but wide-spread raids, so that now, aided by several useful direction-finding devices, they were not incapable of finding and hitting the larger objectives to which they were sent. That at night pin-point accuracy was far from certain mattered little when the principal target was the capital: London was unmissable and the policy to obliterate – *ausradieren*.

In war, and particularly at a decisive moment, there can be little room for sentiment in the decisions of military com-manders; yet, all sentiment excluded, it does not appear possible wholly to accept Churchill's claim, based one must suppose on the views of the air staff, that the continued efficiency of Fighter Command in south-eastern England was 'far more important to us than the protection of London from terror-bombing'. Which is not to say that Churchill was devoid of feeling, far from it. But relative importance had nothing to do with the matter; there was no choice.

The fact is that, although some diminution of the scale of the enemy's assault could be effected by day, against the nightly terror-bombing of London, and of other cities, there was no protection whatever – by Fighter Command or any other branch of air defence. And, however unintentional, there is a hint of callousness about the statement, not confined to Churchill, that Fighter Command experienced a 'sense of relief' at the switch to London on the evening of September 7th. The luckless in-habitants felt no relief. They were not unappreciative of the prolonged and heroic efforts of the fighter pilots to beat off a ruthless enemy, but it is at least open to question whether, had they been given the choice, they would have opted for massacre at night in preference to slaughter by day, even had the day-time casualties been augmented by the failure of Fighter Command in the south-east.

For a time after the mid-September air battles the fate of the nation – and, it may be, the destiny of the world – hung, not upon the ability of the Royal Air Force to fight or to bomb, not upon the Army's renewed strength, nor indeed upon the Navy's unsleeping patrol – for *Sealion* had been postponed – but upon the capacity to resist of the great mass of the ordinary people of London. Their lot was not an enviable one. A timeless passage from Conrad is apt enough to describe it: 'they are not permitted to meditate at ease upon the complicated and acrid savour of existence. They must without pause justify their life to the eternal pity that commands toil to be hard and unceasing, from sunrise to sunset, from sunset to sunrise; till the weary succession of nights and days tainted by the obstinate clamour of sages, demanding bliss and an empty heaven, is redeemed at last by the vast silence of pain and labour, by the dumb fear and the dumb courage of men obscure, forgetful and enduring'. Much glory was theirs; whilst the Navy guarded the moat, they held the keep.

It has been argued that, later in the war, the German people withstood a far heavier bombardment without much flinching. To which it is usually countered that a whole world of difference lay between the two cases, that in Hitler's *Reich* a word of complaint, the least expression of revolt, a thoughtful opinion that the war was lost, and a man might think himself lucky to be hanged without torture; whereas in Britain, it is said, the people could still make their voices heard, could boo or cheer without fear of punishment, could give all or give in; without the basic protection of their liberties, however much curtailed by emergency, they might well have downed tools.

All this may be true enough; but what the ability of the German people to withstand the Anglo-American obliteration bombing of 1944–45 would seem to prove is that had the Luftwaffe, in 1940, been able to carry twice the bomb-load which it then delivered it would still not have caused sufficient moral and material damage to bring about a national surrender. Upon a great nation, well led and determined to hold out, air power could not at that time inflict a knock-out blow.

Both then and later there was talk of the physical exhaustion of fighter pilots – none, be it noted, by the pilots themselves who bitterly resented being pulled out and sent to rest in quieter sectors, and whose zest for flying, matched by their keenness for the fight, certainly kept them going 'from sunrise to sunset' for a 'weary succession' of days. But in fairness it must be remembered that there were others more obscure who at this time were tried to the limits of endurance, those whose toil was often unceasing by day and for whom night brought no respite – and, not least, those in small ships who at all hours and in all weather silently held the sea.

Free to choose, the people of Britain did not hesitate; surrender never entered their heads. On the coasts the great majority stood their ground; many would have fought to the death had the invader landed, for such under Churchill's inspiring leadership was their temper.

And therein lay one of the reasons, military weakness apart, why the chances of even a limited invasion could not be complacently accepted, why the Navy must at all costs bar the way to *Sealion* before a lodgment should be obtained. The German Army might be relied upon to fight honourably if fiercely, but neither honour nor common humanity was to be expected from what followed on – the Nazi administrators, the *Gestapo*, the scum of the self-styled *Herrenvolk*. This could be no restrained and civilized occupation like that of de Ruyter's Dutchmen in 1667, of whom it has been said that 'the Kentish villagers could only regret that the invasion was over when, within the same month, the English soldier, passing through the same districts . . . left a terrible memory in the path he traversed'. In 1940 the 'terrible memory' would have been of German murder and mass deportation. The suggested reversion to the policy of an earlier age that the Army, assisted now by the Air Force, should be responsible for 'holding up the first flight of an invading force' – and that the naval forces in the south should therefore be released for other duties – was, however right in principle, inadmissible in fact at a moment of crisis whose gravity could not accurately be measured. With the Army none too strong and with the greater part of the civilian population remaining upon the threatened coasts, the risks were too fearful. The Navy had to act, and act promptly.

One school of thought has since argued that had the bulk of

cruisers and destroyers detached to the south-eastern seaboard been retained with the Home Fleet they could still have intervened in good time in the Channel once the alarm had been given; and they have cited the example of destroyers from Scapa reaching Dover in twenty hours' steaming at the time of Dunkirk. Stationed with the Home Fleet at Rosyth their approximate steaming time to the Dover area would have been reduced to fifteen hours.

But from twelve to fifteen hours was also the approximate expected duration of the invasion fleet's crossing and, since no earlier warning of the attempt was likely other than visual observation of the departure from the Channel ports, the arrival of forces from Rosyth would, at best, have coincided with the enemy's landing in England. To have missed deliberately the opportunity of intercepting on passage and of sending to the bottom a large part of the 60,000 men in the first echelon might later have seemed regrettable.

Moreover, had the bulk of destroyers and cruisers been released from the Nore they could scarcely have been employed with the Home Fleet without some restriction. Without such restriction they might, at the moment of *Sealion's* departure have been engaged with the fleet upon a chase after the *Hipper* or upon interception of the *Herbstreise*; their steaming time to the south might well have been doubled. On the other hand, had they been held, say, at Rosyth earmarked for anti-invasion duties, the wisdom of keeping them in the north at fifteen hours' steaming rather than in the south at two to three hours from the threatened area would certainly have been open to challenge.

It is of course true that the approximate direction of the enemy's main thrust was not detected until after the first week in September, whereas Admiral Forbes's protests against the serious reduction of his fleet dated from June and July. But the Admiralty's estimate of the Wash-Dover-Newhaven line as the area of probable danger was sufficiently near the mark to permit, without disturbance, a subsequent change of emphasis to the line Dover-Selsey Bill; whilst the policy of vigilant patrolling and immediate interception, if possible on passage, must surely be recognized as wise in the light of General

Brooke's uneasiness concerning the ability of his forces to repel the invader once a lodgment had been gained.

In the event the policy was proved right, though neither the Admiralty nor the Commander-in-Chief Home Fleet could fully appreciate the fact at the time. For it was, above all, the visible presence of British naval forces in the south that finally determined the opinion of the German naval staff. The news that British warships were 'able to operate almost unmolested in the Channel', that patrol vessels were stationed off the coast of France and that over thirty destroyers had been sighted in southern and south-eastern harbours and were 'solely occupied'. together with heavier units of the fleet, 'with this theatre of operations' – in ten days these accumulated observations of British offensive power and intention converted Räder's hesitant optimism ('*Sealion* appears possible') to a forthright opposition that eventually convinced even the German Generals.

Nevertheless, there are some who still hold to the view that the concentrating of anti-invasion flotillas in southern bases was a measure of passive defence and at the same time a denial of the essential flexibility of naval power. Passive it was certainly not; the destroyers off the French coast, together with the aircraft of Bomber Command, were maintaining an *offensive* defence. For the waging of offensive *strategy* Britain had then no means other than the relatively small-scale bombing of German dockyards undertaken at the request of the Admiralty. In England the *Army's* role was *passive* defence, so – despite the fierce daily combats – was that of Fighter Command; both had to wait for the enemy to come to them. Only the destroyers and MTBs supported by the cruisers could impress upon the enemy in his ports that, in the face of 'gunfire and plenty of it', to come out would be to go down.

On the other hand, it was the very flexibility of naval power that enabled ships to be detached from main fleet to face a specific danger elsewhere; once the danger was seen to be averted the same flexibility permitted their return.[1] There was

---

[1] During the second half of October cruisers and destroyers were gradually released from the southern commands, and on November 5th Admiral Forbes brought the Home Fleet ships back to Scapa from Rosyth.

nothing new about these enforced detachments. In 1914 light forces had been taken from the Grand Fleet to Harwich, to guard against an invasion threat that never materialized; even in 1916 the Harwich destroyers were withheld from participation in the battle of Jutland lest the excursion of the High Seas Fleet should cloak some sinister design upon southern England. The difference in 1940 was that, with the menace real, the ships were less numerous and more urgently needed in other sea areas.

What finally appears to emerge is that the temporary weakening of the Home Fleet was both inevitable and, on balance, rewarding.[1] The increased U-boat sinkings to the west of Scotland, due to the lack of escort vessels, were serious; but the presence of light naval forces in the narrow seas had the desired effect. Application of the traditional principal that Britain's first line of defence against invasion must be the enemy's ports brought about the cancellation of the German invasion attempt. Some there were who, for the sake of the deadly injury which a naval and military defeat might have caused Germany that summer, would have preferred to let *Sealion* come out. Somewhat ungenerously, the Royal Navy kept it in.

[1] The detachment, at what was believed to be the height of the invasion crisis, of cruisers and destroyers (apart from battleships from both the Home Fleet and the Mediterranean) for *Operation Menace* (Dakar) appears to be unjustifiable, the more so given the pressing needs of Atlantic convoy. This, however, was a Cabinet not an Admiralty decision.

Appendix A

The Führer and
Supreme Commander
of the Armed Forces

Führer's Headquarters
August 1st, 1940

TOP SECRET   DIRECTIVE No. 17

For the Conduct of Air and Naval Warfare against Britain

In order to establish conditions favourable to the final conquest of Britain, I intend to continue the air and naval war against the British homeland more intensively than heretofore.

With this in mind I issue the following orders:

1. The Luftwaffe is to overcome the British Air Force with all the means at its disposal and in the shortest possible time. The attacks are to be directed primarily against the aircraft themselves, against their ground installations and their supply organizations, also against the aircraft industry, including plants producing anti-aircraft materiel.

2. After we have achieved temporary or local air superiority, the air war is to be carried on against harbours, especially against establishments connected with food supply, and also against similar establishments in the interior of the country.

Attacks on the harbours of the south coast are to be undertaken on the smallest scale possible, in view of our intended operations.

3. On the other hand, air attacks on enemy warships and merchantmen may be diminished, unless particularly advantageous targets offer themselves. . . .

4. The intensified air war is to be carried out in such a manner that the Luftwaffe can be called upon at any time to support naval operations against advantageous targets in sufficient strength. Also, it is to stand by in force for *Operation Sealion*.

5. I reserve for myself the decision on retaliatory terror attacks.

6. The intensified air war may commence on or after August 5th. . . .

The Navy is authorized to begin the projected intensified naval warfare at the same time.

(*signed*) HITLER.

Appendix B

Summary of opinions on the ability of the Luftwaffe to hold off British naval forces operating against *Sealion*, September 1940:

1. GERMAN NAVAL STAFF (*Memorandum*, 19.7.40): 'It cannot be assumed that the Luftwaffe alone will succeed in keeping the enemy naval forces clear of our shipping, as its operations are very dependent on weather conditions ... even if the first wave has been successfully transported, the enemy will still be able to penetrate with resolute naval forces so as to place himself between the first wave, already landed, and the succeeding transports.'

2. RÄDER (*Führer Naval Conference*, 31.7.40): 'The early dawn is the most dangerous time for sea operations, as enemy naval forces ... may have reached the entrance to the Channel by morning without being noticed by our reconnaissance ... even if British naval forces are considerably weakened by air attacks, motor-boats and destroyers can come out in great numbers. ... The Luftwaffe will also not be able to protect the landing effectively at three landing points extending over about 100 kilometres, but will have to concentrate on operating in one area.'

3. GERMAN NAVAL HISTORICAL STAFF (*Appreciation*, 1944): 'It was never even possible to destroy enemy sea superiority by the use of our own air superiority. ... Owing to the weakness of our naval forces, there could be no effective guarantee against the enemy breaking into our area of transports, despite our mine barrages on the flanks and despite our air superiority.'

4. GENERAL SIEWERT (quoted by Liddell Hart, in *The Other Side of the Hill*, as representing von Brauchitsch's views): 'The Navy's heart was not in it, and it was not strong enough to protect the flanks. Neither was the German Air Force strong enough to stop the British Navy.'

5. RUNDSTEDT (quoted by Liddell Hart, *ibid.*): 'The German Navy would have had to control the North Sea as well as the Channel, and was not strong enough to do so. The German Air Force was not sufficient to protect the sea crossing on its own.'

6. LIDDELL HART (*ibid.*): 'Göring expressed assurance that the Luftwaffe could fulfil its part – the double role of dominating the Royal Air Force and checking the Royal Navy's intervention. ... But his confidence was by no means common

among the leaders of the Luftwaffe – Richthofen, who commanded the dive-bombers, was particularly sceptical.'

7. Extract from an appreciation written by VICE-ADMIRAL WEICHOLD (late German Naval Staff) at the end of the war: 'The recognition of this new offensive weapon (*air*), and the temporary German ascendancy in this field led to an underestimation of the influence of British sea power. . . . The operational staff of the Luftwaffe considered that the main target in Britain was the aircraft industry. . . . The directives for this operation expressly stated that sea attacks on warships and shipping must take second place. . . . Effective participation by the Luftwaffe in the war on shipping, which the Navy regarded as the decisive factor against England, did not eventuate.'

Some additional evidence of the inability of the Luftwaffe to keep British warships from the invasion area may be adduced from the activities of the destroyer patrols in the Dover Strait. These destroyers, numbering from ten to twelve each night and supported on various occasions by numerous other ships (vide Chapters 'Ten Nights to Decision'), swept the Franco-Belgian coast throughout September unescorted by British aircraft. Any one of them might, and almost certainly would, have intercepted *Sealion* had it sailed; none of them was attacked on patrol by enemy aircraft.

To this summary Admiral the Hon. Sir Reginald Plunkett-Ernle-Erle-Drax, K.C.B., D.S.O., Commander-in-Chief at the Nore in 1940, has added the following comments:

In general I agree with most of the other opinions that have been expressed to the effect that our Navy would have heavily defeated any German attempt to invade England in 1940. But the defence of Britain was essentially a combined operation of all three services, and in working it out there were various factors of much uncertainty.

The C.-in-C. Home Fleet was naturally reluctant to bring his forces down towards the Channel where they would be exposed to much risk from mines and air attack. The R.A.F., quite understandably, were very reluctant to earmark any air force for co-operation with the Navy on the day of battle; nor could we expect that they would feel free to give direct help to the Navy in repelling invasion. Their bomber forces had done no training to fit them for naval co-operation and they therefore had to point out that if asked to help us they would have been just as likely to bomb our own ships as the enemy's.

R.A.F. fighters would have been invaluable to counter-attack the German bombers, especially the dive-bombers attacking our warships, but they had various other duties to which they attached great importance and there could therefore be no certainty of getting close co-operation at the time and place where we most needed it.

We had many other problems, such as where and when our anti-invasion forces should replenish with fuel and ammunition and land their wounded; what protection against air attack they could be given while in harbour; what minesweepers could be kept working to clear the channels to and from our naval ports such as Harwich, Dover, Sheerness, etc.

It was recognized that our military forces would be so strained that there would be little use in trying to plan detailed co-operation with them, but we should of course have found out the various points where they specially needed our help.

It will be seen from the above that there was inevitably great uncertainty about how the anti-invasion battle would develop and the losses likely to be incurred on both sides. On the whole, however, our available naval strength was amply sufficient for the purpose. Along the whole length of our Channel coast therefore no one had any doubt that, aided by their high morale and splendid offensive spirit, our combined forces would have inflicted a crushing defeat on any invaders that crossed the Channel.

Index

MAPS

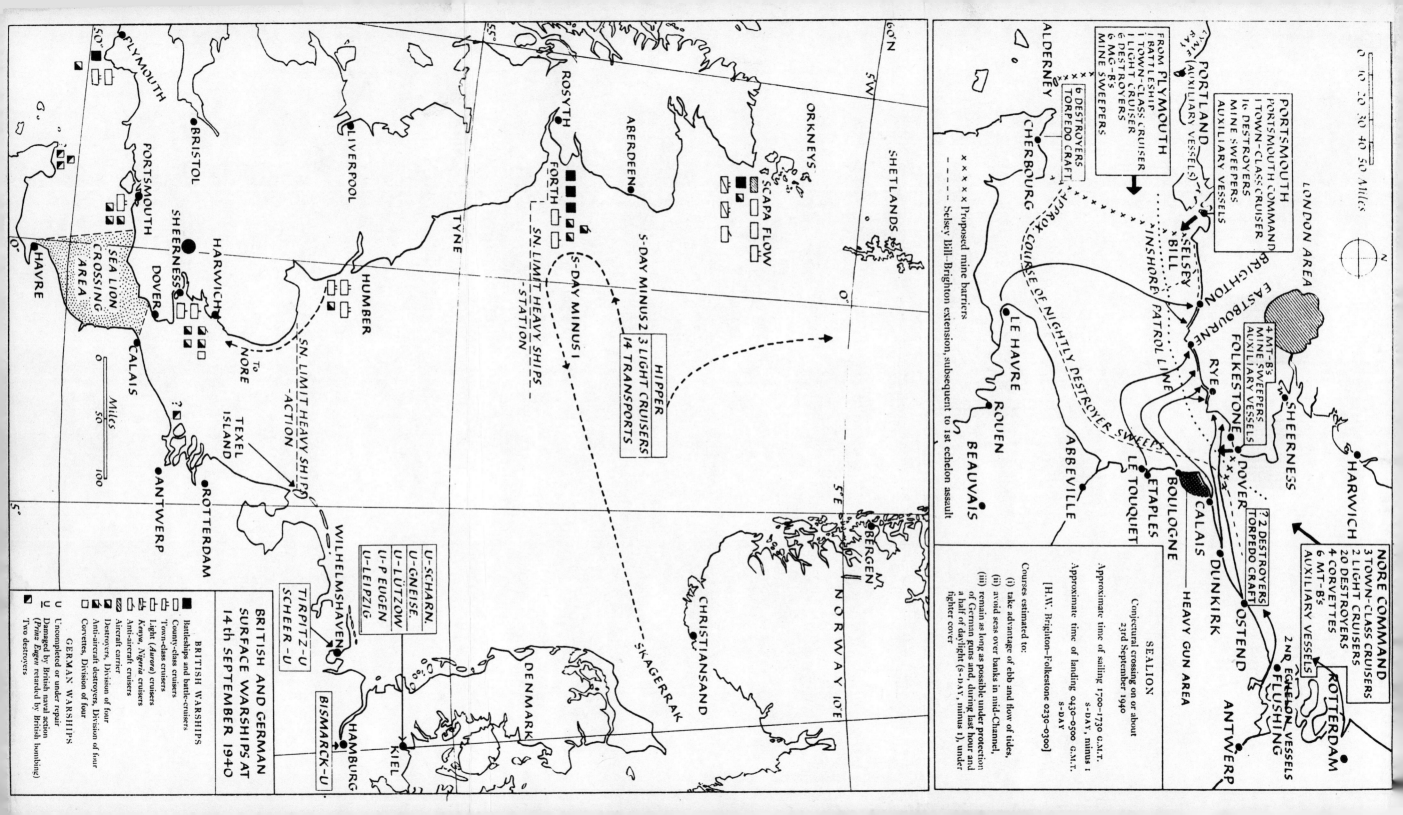

BRITISH AND GERMAN SURFACE WARSHIPS AT 14th SEPTEMBER 1940